The Royal Museum of Fine Arts, Antwerp

Irene Smets

THE ROYAL MUSEUM OF FINE ARTS, ANTWERP
one hundred masterpieces from the collection

Ludion

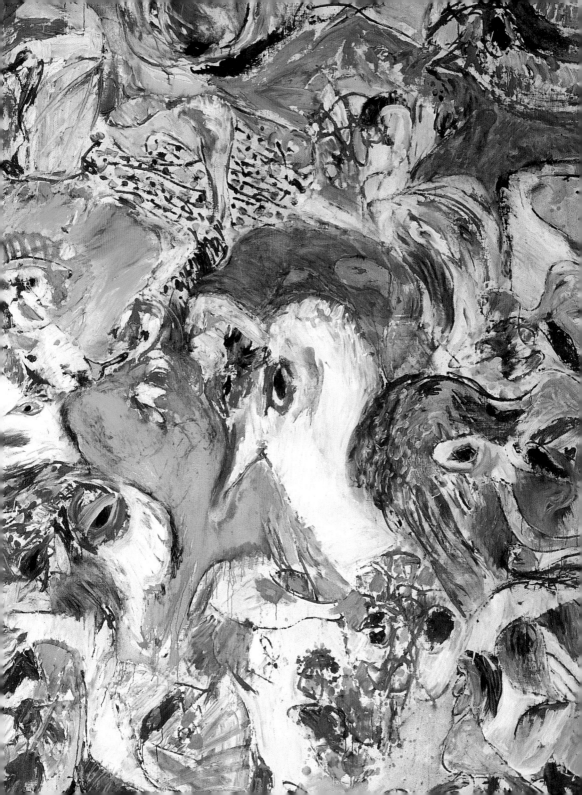

FOREWORD

The Royal Museum in Antwerp has an outstanding collection of fine art. The focus is very much on paintings, although the museum also boasts many marvellous drawings and sculptures. The collection is housed in a fine 19th-century museum building in the heart of Antwerp's South district. The City built this temple of culture in 1883 on the site of the former Zuidkasteel, a fortress which had dominated the area for centuries.

Nowadays, the Flemish Community administers the museum. Its roots go back, however, to the Napoleonic period, when it began life as the museum of a typical municipal academy. During this period, the works of art confiscated under French revolutionary rule were brought together as study materials for students at the academy. Right from the start, therefore, the museum has functioned as a mirror of the historical development of art in Antwerp. The confiscated works included paintings from the gallery of the Guild of St Luke – the traditional painters' corporation – and art treasures that had adorned Antwerp's churches and abbeys for centuries, until their suppression at the end of the 18th century. There were rare paintings that had survived the iconoclastic riots of 1566, masterpieces by Van Orley, Massys, Floris and others, and above all, dozens of altarpieces produced during the Counter-Reformation, the highlights of which were those painted by Rubens and his school. From the outset, Rubens, Van Dyck and Jordaens occupied a special place at the Royal Museum. The jewel in the crown is undoubtedly the Rubens Room, which is reached via a monumental staircase.

The nucleus of the collection, which consisted primarily of late-16th and 17th-century works, was significantly expanded in 1840 with the bequest of Chevalier Florent van Ertborn, who had served as Burgomaster of Antwerp during the period of Dutch rule. His taste – progressive for the time – was for early Netherlandish and quattrocento masters. The bequest gave the museum paintings – now internationally famous – by Van Eyck, Van der Weyden, Memling, Simone Martini, Antonello da Messina and Jean Fouquet. Having been founded in this way, the Old Masters collection was subsequently expanded through donations, bequests and purchases. It now extends, for instance, to a group of leading Dutch masters, including Frans Hals.

In its academic role, the Royal Museum influenced generations of artists in the 19th century. Its development paralleled the vigorous revival of the Port of Antwerp, the new-found prosperity of which stimulated a great deal of artistic activity. The city's academy began to play an important part on the European stage, extending its influence to the Düsseldorf and Hamburg Schools, for instance, and also to Paris. When the elderly Ingres was granted membership of the Antwerp Academy, he donated the customary self-portrait. It turned out to be the last portrait he ever painted. Teachers and students at the academy also regularly donated works to the museum, with the result that the collection of 19th-century masters rapidly began to outnumber those of previous centuries.

At first, the Antwerp baroque – and above all that of Rubens – was the great stylistic inspiration for countless Romantic painters. A good example is the monumental painting by Nicaise de Keyser that adorns the entrance hall. Admiration for the past also opened up new paths, however, and in no way hindered innovation or creativity. The work of Henri de Braekeleer, which is better represented at the Royal Museum than anywhere else, is a perfect illustration.

Towards the end of the 19th century, certain young artists began to react against the academicism of their forebears. These were the painters who laid the foundations of Modernism – an evolution that is also clearly expressed in the museum's collection. Thanks to a number of important donations, including that of François Franck, the Royal Museum has the world's finest Ensor collection and has also acquired the richest body of Rik Wouters' work. A fascinating collection of modern art was gradually formed, including paintings by Flemish Impressionists, Symbolists, Surrealists, Expressionists, Intimists and Abstract artists – great names like Gustave van de Woestyne, Jakob Smits, Constant Permeke, Jean Brusselmans, René Magritte and Jozef Peeters. Not to mention key foreign artists like Grosz and Modigliani, many of whom are represented by exceptionally fine works.

This book, with its hundred featured works, will serve as your guide, helping you to see the works in a clearer and more coherent way. I hope that it will contribute to an enjoyable and instructive visit.

Dr. Paul Huvenne, Chief Curator

1382	Antwerp's artists found the Guild of St Luke. The guild's own paintings are kept in a 'constkamer' or gallery
1663	The painter David Teniers is among the guild members who found a new Academy of Fine Art
1773	Dissolution of the guild: the works from the 'constkamer' are handed on to the academy
1810	The academy and the museum move into a former Franciscan abbey
1815	The collection is expanded by the return of works confiscated by the French in the 1790s from public buildings and suppressed monasteries and churches. These include paintings by Rubens
1815–30	King William I donates several important works during the period of Dutch rule
19–20th C	Numerous gifts and bequests
1840	Priceless bequest (including Flemish Primitives) of Chevalier Florent van Ertborn, former burgomaster of Antwerp
1851	Foundation of the 'Academisch Korps' for talented artists. Each new member has to donate a self-portrait to the museum
1859	Van den Hecke-Baut de Rasmon bequest (chiefly 17th-century Flemish and Dutch masters)
1864	Foundation of the 'Artibus Patriae' association to acquire works for the museum
1873	Appointment of an Acquisition Committee
1884–90	Construction of a new museum in Antwerp's South district (architects Jean-Jacques Winders and Frans Van Dijck)
1927	Ownership of the museum passes to the Belgian State
1926–99	Collection expands thanks to the 'Friends of Modern Art' society and benefactors like Louis, François and Charles Franck, and Ludo van Bogaert-Sheid

The collection of the Royal Museum of Fine Arts in Antwerp currently totals around 7,200 works of art – including 3,200 paintings, 3,300 drawings and prints, and 400 sculptures.

Angel Gabriel, Virgin Mary,
Christ Wounded by the Lance,
Descent from the Cross c. 1340

Simone Martini c. 1284–1344
Panel, 23 x 14 cm and 24 x 15 cm
Four (originally two) panels from a Passion polyptych

These paintings originally formed two panels that were subsequently sawn in half to separate the images on the front and back. The *Angel Gabriel* came from the rear of the panel with *Christ Wounded by the Lance*, while the *Virgin Mary* appeared on the back of the *Descent from the Cross*. They belonged to a polyptych – possibly a 'travelling altar' – devoted to the Passion of Christ. The Louvre in Paris and Berlin's Staatliche Museen have other panels from the same work – *Christ Carrying the Cross* and the *Entombment*. The frames of *Christ Carrying the Cross*, *Christ Wounded with the Lance* and the *Descent from the Cross* are inscribed with the words HOC OPUS – PINXIT – SYMON. When the polyptych was closed, the figures of Gabriel and Mary were united in an Annunciation scene.

Simone Martini worked for most of his life in his native Siena and in one or two other Italian cities. In 1339, he moved to Avignon to work at the papal court. These paintings were probably done in the Provençal city on behalf of an important prelate – presumably the bishop whose small figure kneels in the foreground in the *Descent*. The little altar was extremely precious in terms of its raw materials alone – Martini used gold leaf and ultramarine, both of which were very costly. In certain areas of the polyptych he painted over the gold leaf to produce colours with a special transparency. Ultramarine was made from the semiprecious stone lapis lazuli, which was imported from Asia via Venice and produced the most beautiful blue pigment.

As was customary, the painting was executed in tempera rather than oils, which only became popular later. Tempera is a form of paint in which egg-white, egg-yolk or diluted glue is used as a binder for the pigments.

The respective scenes, each set against a golden background, show extraordinary refinement in their decorative, yet highly expressive, presentation. Martini's dreamy, sentimental style and his refined design and colouring make him a characteristic representative of Sienese painting in the 14th century.

installed at Utrecht's Church of St John in 1363 to commemorate the priest Hendrik van Rijn.

This very early Crucifixion illustrates the style of painting in the Low Countries before 1400, prior to the era of Jan van Eyck. Several characteristic features of the 'International Style' or 'courtly Gothic', as it is sometimes known, are in evidence here. They include this serene Christ and the stylised figures, which, with the exception of their heads, hands and a glimpse of foot, are enveloped in the drapery of their robes. Other typical elements are their S-shaped poses, weightless appearance, gentle and pensive expressions and the lack of characterisation in the face of the donor, who is rendered impersonally and in profile.

The sun and the moon in the upper corners are ancient motifs from popular art. In this case, however, they may also allude to Gospel passages like 'darkness came over the whole land... while the sun's light failed'.

If we compare this panel with the museum's 'Flemish Primitives' collection – works by artists like Van Eyck, Van der Weyden, Memling and David – it is plain how rapidly painting was to develop in the decades that followed.

The crucified Christ is flanked by his mother and his disciple John, who lays a protective hand on a figure kneeling in prayer at the foot of the Cross, as if wishing to present him to his master. This is the donor of the painting: custom required that he be shown much smaller than the divine company in which he appears. The purpose of this memorial panel is revealed by the Latin inscription at the bottom. It was

St Romuald Refuses Emperor Otto III   Fra Angelico c. 1400–1455
Entry into the Church   Panel, 22 x 27 cm
second half 15th century

order that St Romuald founded near Florence around 1000 AD. This painting may have belonged to an altarpiece devoted to the holy abbot, as there was a revival in the cult of St Romuald in Tuscany in the second half of the 15th century.

Although the panel has all the characteristics of Fra Angelico's charming and ethereal style, some experts nevertheless attribute it to one of the master's disciples and date it to shortly after his death. Fra Angelico (Guido di Pietro), 'Il Beato', was a Dominican monk who spent the period 1439–1445 at the monastery of San Marco in Florence, where he painted his celebrated frescos. His contemporaries greatly admired him for his carefully conceived and spiritual rendering of religious subjects.

St Romuald is dressed as an abbot and holds a stick in his hand in an almost threatening manner, preventing the emperor from entering a church. Otto had committed a number of crimes, including murder and adultery, and was required to make a public act of penance before he could be admitted: his contrite pose expresses his feelings of remorse. His companions include a dwarf who, with comic aplomb, places the emperor's sword beside him on the ground, which may allude to the impotence of worldly rulers when set against the might of the Church. In the distance on the right we see several monks of the Camaldolite

St Barbara was the daughter of a wealthy pagan who, wishing to protect her from the outside world, locked her up in a tower. Even so, he could not prevent her from coming into contact with Christianity. She converted and had a triple window installed in the tower to symbolise her devotion to the Holy Trinity. When her father discovered what she had done, he had her tortured in the hope of breaking her faith. Finally, he beheaded his daughter with his own hands, upon which he was struck by lightning.

One of the most popular saints in the Middle Ages, St Barbara was usually depicted with her tower. In this case, she wears a robe with broad folds and holds a prayerbook and her martyr's palm. She is sitting in front of a fine Late Gothic tower, in which we can clearly see the triple window. The book symbolises her faith and the palm her spiritual victory. Masons and stonecutters are hard at work around the tower, and a group of people is approaching on horseback, while several others stand and talk. A deep landscape is visible in the background.

Jan van Eyck's inscription on the imitation marble frame states that he produced the work in 1437. It displays various characteristics of his style – the skilful way he captured nature and architecture, his sense of symbolism, the detail and technical refinement, and the ability to create a coherent and entirely convincing image of a metaphysical world.

St Barbara is not a painting. It could be the underdrawing of an unfinished panel, or a drawing in its own right. The image was done in silverpoint on a smooth, yellowish-brown preparatory layer and was then finished with a fine paintbrush. The fact that he signed and dated it suggests that Van Eyck probably viewed it as finished, though we cannot be certain. When the panel and frame were cut from the same board, as is the case here, the artist would sometimes complete the frame, including the date, before finishing the painting.

Jan van Eyck is believed to have been born near Maaseik, in the modern Belgian province of Limburg. In 1425, he was appointed painter to the court of Philip the Good, Duke of Burgundy, which was renowned for its splendour. He moved to Bruges in 1432 and died there nine years later. His most famous painting is the *Adoration of the Lamb* (1432), which he painted for Ghent's Cathedral of St Bavo, probably in collaboration with his brother Hubert.

According to the calligraphic text at the bottom of the original frame, Jan van Eyck painted this Virgin and Child in 1439. Above it, he added his motto *Als ich kan* ('to the best of my ability').

Van Eyck was one of the first Flemish Primitives – the artists who introduced the meticulous observation of people and the world, and the new technique of oil painting, into 15th-century Netherlandish art. Van Eyck used these skills to create a perfect universe, in which earthly reality is a manifestation of a higher world. This little panel is a good example. Mary and her baby stand in a heavenly garden. Every detail is true to life and painted with immense care. At the same time, the artist evokes a mystical reality, the Enclosed Garden or *Hortus Conclusus*. The fountain, the rosebush, the lily-of-the-valley and the iris are all symbols of the Virgin Mary: to medieval people, creation was full of references to the divine.

The dukes of Burgundy preferred to reside in Flanders – Bruges, Ghent and Brussels – and Flemish artists benefited significantly from the patronage of the court. Bruges, the capital of the County of Flanders, was also home to a prosperous bourgeoisie, which liked to show off its wealth by commissioning works of art. Another major patron was the Church – an institution at the height of its powers that dominated every aspect of society. This was the background against which the Flemish Primitives produced their art.

Rogier van der Weyden built his reputation with two sets of works. The first was a series of altarpieces featuring episodes from the Passion, in which the crucified Christ is surrounded by highly emotional figures. The second consisted of perceptive portraits of the Burgundian nobility and Flemish bourgeoisie. This image of Philippe de Croÿ is a model of the stylistic refinement displayed by the Tournai-Brussels master, which transforms the human face into a brilliant artistic form from which every superfluous element has been stripped. The restrained expression, serene composition, soft colouring against a dark background and the velvet tunic all suggest that De Croÿ was a cultivated and pious nobleman, while the fine gold neck chain defuses any sense of severity.

The sitter was governor of Hainaut and a member of the Duke of Burgundy's entourage. The monogram in the upper left corner refers to his title 'Seigneur de Sempy'. His prayerful pose may indicate that this panel was once the right wing of a diptych, with a Virgin and Child or some other devotional image on the left.

The portrait dates from between 1452 and 1460, when Philippe de Croÿ was still a young man.

Sacrament Altarpiece

Rogier van der Weyden
(and workshop) *c.* 1399–1464
Panel, 200 x 97 cm (central panel),
119 x 63 cm (wings)

Rogier van der Weyden uses this altarpiece to illustrate the Seven Sacraments. The images are set in a Gothic church, with a Crucifixion scene in the middle. The importance of this central event, positioned right in the foreground with Jesus raised high on the Cross, is emphasised by the size of the figures compared to those in the wings. The dramatic yet restrained eloquence of the little group at the foot of the Cross is typical of Van der Weyden. It comprises the disciple John, who supports Jesus' mother as she faints with distress, and several grieving women. Rogier differs in this respect from his direct Flemish Primitive forebear Jan van Eyck, whose figures are in perfect emotional equilibrium. The moulding of their bodies, which gives them a sense of sculptural volume, is also typical of Van der Weyden's art.

The representation of the Seven Sacraments is attractively arranged around the aisles and choir of the church. Each one is identified by an angel with a banderole (scroll). Beginning in the left aisle, we see Baptism, with a white angel representing innocence regained. Confirmation is symbolised by a yellow angel (the holy fire of faith) and Confession by a red angel (burning repentance). At the back of the right aisle a priest is being ordained, accompanied by a dark purple angel (kingship), followed by Marriage with a blue angel (loyalty) and Extreme Unction with a black angel (mourning). At the high altar in the central panel, a priest raises the host during mass, watched over by a green angel (vitality). There are many fascinating details in addition

to the Sacraments, such as the beggars at the church door on the far left of the central panel, and the dogs, which are symbols of loyalty. The interior of the church itself is also well worth studying. As in Van Eyck's work, the rich colours result from the skilful application of successive layers of translucent oil paint.

Jean Chevrot, bishop of Tournai, probably commissioned the triptych in 1441 for his private chapel. Van der Weyden included him in the painting as the bishop in the Confirmation scene.

Surprisingly, several of the heads (undoubtedly portraits) were painted on tin foil and then pasted onto the panel. The paint is thicker here and there are fewer cracks. The facial features are slightly blurred and a little cruder than the others. The heads of the priest at the baptismal font, the man with the red tunic and the figure with the black hat just behind him were all inserted in this way, as were a number of others. Perhaps they were added later by another artist.

Rogier van der Weyden (Rogier de le Pasture) was born in Tournai, where he trained as a painter. He later worked in Brussels as the official municipal artist. He had a workshop in the city with many assistants, who will undoubtedly have had a hand in a large altarpiece like this. The influence of his compositions persisted in Western art for centuries.

Christ Giving his Blessing,
with Angels Singing
and Playing Instruments 1489

Hans Memling c. 1440–1494
Panel, 164 x 212 cm (central panel),
165 x 230 cm (wings)
Fragments from the high altar
of Santa Maria la Real, Nájera, Spain
Wings: *Musical angels*

of Castile and León. The overall scene is set against a band of clouds that runs across all three panels.

The unsigned altarpiece is generally attributed to Hans Memling, possibly, in view of the large scale of the commission, with the assistance of his workshop.

Memling was a key figure in the continuing development of the new painting style that arose in the Southern Netherlands in the 15th

This image of Christ with a group of angels used to be part of a gigantic altarpiece in a Spanish abbey. The complete work also included the Assumption and Coronation of the Virgin with life-size saints, apostles and martyrs, but all of that is now lost. The altarpiece as a whole was intended to glorify Christ and his mother.

The three surviving monumental panels focus on the King of Heaven. His costume is simultaneously the crown and royal cloak of a monarch and the tiara and cope of a High Priest. He holds a crystal orb with a large cross, symbolising the Christian realm. The large clasp with three precious stones refers to the Holy Trinity – the Father, the Son and the Holy Spirit.

The six angels arranged on either side of the Christ figure form a three-part choir. The other two panels each contain five angels playing more or less all the instruments that were used in the 15th-century Netherlands to perform liturgical music. The angels on the left play a psaltery, tromba marina, lute, trumpet and oboe, and those on the right a straight trumpet, regular trumpet, portative organ, harp and fiddle.

The angels' robes and instruments are minutely detailed, including a lily (emblem of the abbey at Nájera) and the three towers and the lion of the kings

century. An important feature of 'Flemish Primitive' art, as it has been christened, is its blending of optical realism and mysticism. Like Van Eyck and Van der Weyden before him, Memling offered a precisely detailed and 'human' visualisation of the divine world: in this example, the angels' liturgical robes are rendered with amazing realism. However, the restrained and somewhat sentimental style creates a

We do not know a great deal about the life of **Hans Memling**. 'Meester Hans' came from the German town of Seligenstadt on the river Main. Having trained in Germany and, possibly, under Rogier van der Weyden in Brussels, he settled permanently in Bruges, where his prestige grew steadily year by year.

sense of unreality in many of Memling's paintings, as in a vision or a 'Late Gothic dream'.

Hans Memling began to work as a painter in Bruges around 1465. His patrons included churches and abbeys, rich burghers and foreign merchants – especially Italians – who were active in the city. This painting is an example of such a commission, although we do not know the man's identity. He holds an antique Roman coin, with the head of Emperor Nero, which may suggest that he was a coin collector. His clothes are in the late 15th-century Italian style and his features are Mediterranean, both of which could indicate that he was an Italian. The style of the portrait, which reflects the spirit of the early Italian Renaissance, may also point in that direction. The man looks directly at the viewer, which is unusual in a portrait by Memling. However, his gaze is rather dreamy and introverted, and does not really make contact with the outside world.

Although the figure occupies most of the picture area, the landscape in the background is rendered with great care. Several details in it may be clues as to the sitter's identity, including the palm tree, the man on the white horse and the swans. The laurel leaves bottom centre are also intriguing, as they undoubtedly refer in one way or another to the name or emblem of the man immortalised in this mysterious portrait.

*Mary and Jesus with Seraphim
and Cherubim c. 1451–1452*

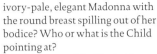

Jean Fouquet *c.* 1420–1480
Panel, 94.5 x 85.5 cm
Right wing of a diptych

This painting by the French artist
Jean Fouquet is one of the most
striking in the museum. The image,
with its unreal colours and cool
presence, is intriguing yet alienat-
ing. Nowhere else are we made to
realise quite so clearly that the mental world of our ancestors is often a
closed book to us. Who is this
ivory-pale, elegant Madonna with
the round breast spilling out of her
bodice? Who or what is the Child
pointing at?

This image of the Virgin Mary
embodies the 15th-century ideal of
beauty: a young woman with a white
skin and hairless face, lowered eyes,
round breasts and narrow waist. Her
features are traditionally said to be
those of Agnès Sorel, who was mis-
tress of King Charles VII of France
and who died of poisoning in 1450.

The royal treasurer, Etienne
Chevalier, commissioned the painting from the court artist, Jean Fouquet, shortly after that date. It was
originally part of a diptych, the left
wing of which featured Chevalier
himself with St Stephen, his patron
saint (now in the museum at
Berlin). Laboratory tests have
shown that the Antwerp and Berlin
panels were painted on wood from
the same tree.

Nine little angels – six red and
three blue – surround Mary's
throne. They are traditionally identified as seraphim (the fiery-red figures) and cherubim (blue like the
air), although many other interpre-
tations are also possible. It has been
suggested, for instance, that they
symbolise love (red) and purity
(blue), day and night, good and evil,
the nine angelic choirs, and so on.
The fact that only the red angels are
permitted to touch the throne may
also be significant.

Christ hangs serenely from the Cross, which stands precisely at the centre of the composition, between the two thieves, whose contorted bodies are tied to tree trunks. The artist has taken the opportunity to present three studies of the human body. The background contains a landscape beneath a clear sky, rather than the storms we find in corresponding paintings elsewhere in the museum, like Rubens' *Crucifixion* and *Christ Wounded by the Lance*, and Van Dyck's *Crucifixion*. The attractive panorama contrasts with the rocky foreground, in which the anguished Mary and St John have slumped to the ground among the bones and skulls.

Several elements in the panels are symbols of death and salvation: the snakes that crawl around the skulls, the long-eared owl (a night bird), the branch growing from the tree trunk, the deer (symbols of the pious soul) and the lily-of-the-valley, which alludes to love and to heaven.

A sheet of parchment (*cartellino*) is attached to the stump of a cross in the left foreground. The inscription reads *1475 antonellus messaneus me pinxit*. Antonello da Messina's work successfully combined the chief characteristics of 15th-century Flemish and Italian painting. In this *Calvary*, for instance, the landscape with the horsemen riding away, the symbols and the attention to detail are typically Flemish, while the plastic rendering of the tormented figures, the wide, open space and the southern light are full of the spirit of Italian Renaissance painting.

Antonello da Messina came from Sicily. During his training in Naples, he is sure to have seen many of the Flemish paintings (by Jan van Eyck, Rogier van der Weyden and Petrus Christus, among others) commissioned by Italian patrons in the Low Countries. He may even have travelled to Flanders himself. Either way, he was strongly influenced by the Flemish Primitives. When he subsequently worked in Venice, he learned a great deal from the artists active in that city, while they in turn picked up the technique of oil painting, which da Messina had borrowed from Flemish artists. Working in oils offered richer and glossier colours than the hitherto customary tempera. This *Calvary* is one of the earliest oil paintings by an Italian artist.

Portrait of the Artist and his Wife 1496   Master of Frankfurt
1460–early 16th century
Panel, 38 x 26 cm

Archery Festival: detail with the 'self-portrait' of the Master of Frankfurt.

It is generally assumed that this is a portrait of the artist and his wife. The man appears in a similar pose in several paintings attributed to the Master of Frankfurt – including the *Archery Festival*, where he can be made out just below the centre and a little to the right, wearing a brown robe and a cap.

The couple sit at a table, possibly symbolising their married status. Notice the two realistically painted flies, both of which appear on the woman's side of the painting. Their significance is unclear: they are disproportionately large, which gives them the appearance of sitting on the panel. Perhaps this was the intention and the viewer is meant to try to chase them away. The little flowers, the flies and the still life of bread and berries seem like a deliberate display of the artist's virtuosity.

The panel is dated 1496 and also features the numbers 36 and 27, which may be the ages of the two sitters. If so, we can calculate the year in which the Master of Frankfurt was born. The arms of the Antwerp Painters' Guild feature at the top. The work is one of the first non-religious double portraits in 15th-century Flemish art.

There are traces of hinges on the side of the black and gold frame, suggesting that the painting once belonged to a larger ensemble – a diptych or perhaps even a decorated cabinet.

The museum has a second work by the Master of Frankfurt – the aforementioned *Archery Festival* – which dates from around 1493. It is an enigmatic painting that incorporates all kinds of symbols and allegorical elements.

The Master of Frankfurt was an anonymous Netherlandish master who was active in Antwerp around 1500. The name given him by art historians reflects the fact that his two most important panels were painted for patrons from Frankfurt-am-Main. He may possibly have been Hendrik van Wueluwe, a painter active in Antwerp in this period.

Diptych of Christiaan de Hondt 1499   Master of 1499
Panel, 31 x 14.5 cm
Reverse: *Christ Giving his Blessing* and
Robrecht de Clercq

The left wing has a Virgin and Child in a Gothic church, while the one on the right shows the patron at prayer in a cosy medieval interior. Christiaan de Hondt was the Cistercian abbot of Ter Duinen Abbey on the Flemish coast between 1495 and 1509. Robrecht de Clercq, the monk shown kneeling on the reverse of the panel, was appointed abbot of the same abbey a few years later. His portrait dates from after 1515 and is by a different painter.

It is plain from Mary's crown and Abbot de Hondt's mitre and staff that the Master of 1499 liked to paint precious materials and jewels. The dog ('hond' in Dutch) may refer to the donor's surname. The little devotional diptych against the rear wall of the alcove is an interesting detail – it is as if the artist were indicating where his finished painting should be placed in the abbot's quarters.

This sleeping area is painted in azurite – a pigment that was difficult to use and was applied thickly over a dark preparatory layer in order to achieve the strongest optical effect. Zones painted in azurite are raised slightly, making them especially vulnerable when a panel is cleaned. The strange, unstructured azure-blue colour of the alcove may be the result of pigment degeneration or of careless cleaning.

The Master of 1499 belonged to the 'Flemish Primitive' tradition. This is the only one of the works ascribed to him to have been dated, hence the name that art historians use to identify him.

combines with the subtly varied brushwork to produce brilliant colour combinations and refined lighting effects across the entire surface.

The painting refers to a political and military episode in 1502, when a Catholic army recaptured the island of Santa Maura from the Turks. Bishop Jacopo Pesaro, commander of the papal fleet, defeated the Turks in a naval battle with his Venetian and Spanish allies. He is shown kneeling respectfully, dressed in the robe of a Knight of Malta and holding the standard of the Borgia family. The helmet on the ground before him is an allusion to his military status. The standing figure at his side is Pope Alexander VI (Rodrigo Borgia), who died in 1503. Pesaro probably commissioned the painting from Titian shortly after Alexander's death as a tribute to the late pope and to the papal office personified by St Peter.

Titian (Tiziano di Gregorio Vecellio) trained in Venice and worked there for the whole of his life. His substantial body of work is considered to belong to the High Renaissance and includes religious and mythological scenes, together with countless portraits. Many artists, including those in the Southern Netherlands, were influenced by his treatment of light and colour and his vision of the landscape. The Venetian master was an immense inspiration to Anthony van Dyck, among others.

All the characteristic features of the mature Titian can be found in this early work: the rich colours, the lovely rendering of materials and the intense expression of the two figures on the right.

The painting's recent restoration included the removal of old layers of varnish and discoloured overpainting, revealing a number of interesting physical facts in the process; it was found, for instance, that the artist laid down the colours in several layers using a limited number of high-quality pigments. This

Mary Magdalene stands in front of a portico with porphyry columns, which looks out across a distant landscape between two large buildings. We can identify her from her attribute, the open ointment jar. According to the Bible, she was a repentant sinner who washed Christ's feet with her tears and dried them with her hair, before anointing them with balsam from an alabaster pot.

Mary is shown half-figure within an imaginary triangle, the base of which coincides with her left forearm. The curvature of her head is echoed in the arch of the portico, which, together with the column and capital on the right, matches the curved shape of the panel. The studied composition gives the overall image a strong sense of harmony. This balance and the spatial effects reflect the new artistic ideas of the Renaissance, while the Magdalene embodies contemporary ideals of beauty.

Massys lived in the transitional era between the Late Middle Ages, when the Netherlands were still under Burgundian rule, and the Early Modern era, when the Habsburgs came to power. It was the time of Mary of Burgundy, Philip the Fair, Emperor Charles V, the great voyages of discovery, Leonardo da Vinci and Michelangelo, Erasmus' *Praise of Folly* (1511), Martin Luther and Albrecht Dürer's tour of the Low Countries (1520–21).

The Lamentation 1508–11

Quentin Massys *c.* 1466–1530
Panel, 260 x 263 cm (central panel), 260 x 120 cm (wings)
Altarpiece of the Cabinetmakers' Guild at the Church of Our Lady in Antwerp
(wings) *Salome Presents the Head of St John the Baptist* (left)
and *St John the Evangelist in the Boiling Oil*
(closed shutters) *St John the Baptist* (left) and *St John the Evangelist*

Nine figures are grouped around the dead Christ at the foot of Golgotha, preparing the body for the entombment. Mary Magdalene uses her long hair to wipe the blood from Jesus' feet and Christ's mother, Mary, is supported by the apostle John. The tomb itself is visible in the rocks behind. A maid is sweeping the floor, while another woman holds up a light. And these are by no means the only fascinating details – the wings too are full of them. On the left, set in a Renaissance interior, we see the episode from the Bible in which the severed head of St John the Baptist is presented to King Herod and his lover Herodias by the latter's daughter, Salome. The right wing has a torture scene, in which St John the Evangelist stands in a cauldron of boiling oil, surrounded by a large group of tormentors, whose wickedness is written all over their faces. No fewer than five horses are crammed into the crowd. Antwerp's riverside fortress, Het Steen, looms up in the background.

In this monumental triptych, Massys enriches the Flemish tradition with new Italian ideas concerning the treatment of light and colour, space and volume. Traditional elements include the theme, the composition and the typology of the main figures (inspired by Rogier van der Weyden). The Italian influence, meanwhile, is chiefly apparent in the landscape, certain architectural features in the left wing and, above all, in some of the

figures. The graceful Salome, for instance, recalls the work of Leonardo da Vinci.

Towards the end of the 15th century, as the fame of the Flemish Primitives began to diminish, many artists began to settle in the flourishing commercial metropolis of Antwerp. A new style of painting began to develop in that milieu, which blended native and Italian elements. **Quentin Massys** was the first important figure of the emergent Antwerp school. He trained as a painter in his native Louvain – probably in the workshop of Dieric Bouts – and moved north to Antwerp around 1490. His early work is still rooted in the Flemish Primitive tradition, but he later drew inspiration from the Italian Renaissance. The museum has six paintings by this artist.

Joachim Patinir *c.* 1480–1524
Panel, 17 x 21 cm

Patinir painted imaginary landscapes with high viewpoints and successive planes of depth leading off to the horizon. He used the sequence of brown, green and hazy blue to create a highly atmospheric effect. The human figures, which often convey a religious theme, are merely a pretext for creating a 'world landscape'. They are often tiny, making the natural scene appear even more expansive and the distance even more infinite.

Like many artists of his day, Patinir, who was born in the Dinant area, settled in Antwerp. He was a good friend of Quentin Massys, with whom he regularly collaborated: Patinir painted the landscape and Massys added the figures, assuming that they were larger than those in the small panel here.

The Holy Family trudges along in the foreground, past a clump of trees. Close by, the image of an idol topples spontaneously from its pedestal. In the right middle ground we see a pond and a few farm buildings, around which the Massacre of the Innocents in Bethlehem is unfolding. The wide world beyond is devoid of human activity.

The artist's *trompe-l'oeil* signature is carved into the rock in the left foreground: OPUS JOACHIM D. PATINIR.

The Martyrdom of St Catherine

Jan Provost c. 1465–1529
Panel, 94 x 68 cm
Right wing of a triptych
(reverse) *St Barbara*

A somewhat misshapen execution-
er raises his sword to cut off St
Catherine's head. A crowd of people
has gathered around, some on foot,
others on horseback. It is all but
impossible to make out precisely
how many horses are crammed into
the panel – Jan Provost certainly
succeeded in creating the effect of a
large and confused mass.

The colourful scene contains elements of both tradition and renew-
al. The theme is an old one, illustrat-
ing the persistence of late medieval
piety in Flemish painting, while the
realistic horse's head on the right
and the lively rendering of the figures are typical of the artistic evolution of the period. Provost belonged
to the circle of Quentin Massys and
other artists who were receptive to
Italian influences. After a few years,
however, he left Antwerp and settled in Bruges.

This panel may have belonged to
a triptych with scenes from the life
of St Catherine. The central panel
has been lost. The other wing, with
*St Catherine Disputing with the
Emperor and the Fifty Philosophers,*
is now in the Boijmans Van Beunin-
gen Museum in Rotterdam.

Bernard van Orley c. 1488–1541
Panel, 248 x 218 cm (central panel), 248 x 94 cm (wings)
Triptych for the municipal almoners of Antwerp
(wings) *Three Works of Mercy* (left) and *Three Works of Mercy* (right)
(closed wings) *St Stephen and St Mark* (left)
and *St Laurence and St Elizabeth* (right)

The seventh work of mercy, burying the dead, is shown in the central panel. It provides the focus for a grandiose Last Judgement, with a mass of animated, naked figures who witness the Second Coming of Christ, enabling the painter to show the human body in a wide variety of poses. In this work, Bernard van Orley displays his enthusiasm for the new art from Italy – that of Raphael and Michelangelo. At this stage it was known in the Netherlands only from drawings and prints, yet had already sparked off a fully fledged artistic revolution.

The classical buildings and studied perspective in the wings testify to the same spirit. The left wing shows three works of mercy: giving drink to the thirsty, visiting the sick and harbouring strangers. The remaining three works appear on the right: feeding the hungry, clothing the naked and ministering to prisoners. We also see a group of people tending to a dying man.

The earth is separated from heaven by a band of clouds running across the three panels. The inhabitants of the zone beyond the clouds are also gripped with excitement about the unfolding events, as we see from the individual and expressive pose that the painter has given each figure. The centre of the entire work – the vanishing point of its perspective system – is the angel who descends to announce the Day of Judgement.

Bernard van Orley ran the most important painter's workshop in

Van Orley used azurite to obtain the dark blue of the robes. This colour was always applied over another, darker layer of paint, which made it somewhat thicker; its structure is also relatively granular. There are fairly obvious examples here in the robe worn by the Virgin Mary, seated in heaven on the far left, and in the drapery of the canopy in the right wing.

Brussels and was court painter to Margaret of Austria and her successor Mary of Hungary, both of whom served as governors of the Netherlands on behalf of Emperor Charles v.

Jean Clouet was born in the Southern Netherlands and moved to France around 1500, becoming court painter to King François I. All his surviving works are portraits, a field in which he was exceptionally gifted. He produced a famous series of portraits in black and red chalk of princes and princesses, fools, knights, courtiers and ladies-in-waiting (in the Musée Condé, Chantilly).

This small panel shows a royal child that history has more or less forgotten – the short-lived heir of François I. The dauphin was born in 1518 and died in 1536, at the age of 18. He cannot be older than four or five here (note the hand in particular). The portrait may thus be dated to around 1522.

This is an idealised image of the little prince. Dressed ceremonially, he is an assured and dignified presence, entirely in keeping with the rules of traditional courtly art. In spite of these restrictions, the artist has managed to produce a sensitive and lively child's portrait.

Judith　　　　　　Jan Massys c. 1509–1575
　　　　　　　　　Panel, 115 x 80 cm

Jan and Cornelis, the sons of Quentin Massys, followed their father's example – both became painters of religious and moralising themes, landscapes and genre scenes. The story of Judith comes from the Bible. To save her city, she seduced and then murdered the enemy general, Holofernes.

Stylistically, Jan Massys' panel is related to the Fontainebleau school, which arose in France in the 16th century, when King François I ordered the construction of Fontainebleau château. To decorate the interior, he recruited a group of Italian, French and Flemish artists, who developed a cool, elegant and mannered style. Judith's sensual nudity, veiled in gauze, and her prominent jewellery are both typical of the Fontainebleau school of painting.

The artist signed his work on the sword: JOANNES MASSIIS PING.

Lucas Cranach the Elder's nudes are immediately recognisable: the same type recurs time and again in his many mythological and religious images. Cranach remained rooted in the formal idiom of the Middle Ages rather than in Renaissance art, which drew its inspiration from classical sculpture. That is not to say, however, that Cranach closed his eyes to the new art. The elegance of this 'earthly' little figure in its almost invisible veil of gauze bears witness to the modern spirit, as does the allegorical theme.

Caritas – charity – is presented as a young mother sitting beneath an apple tree with her three children. The way she suckles the smallest child actually makes her more of a personification of motherly love than of fellow feeling. The background is like a stage set, little attention has been paid to perspective and the figures are rendered in a very graphic style, all of which is typical of this German master.

Lucas Cranach the Elder worked in Wittenberg as court painter to Frederick the Wise, the Elector of Saxony. He ran a large workshop and served at one stage as burgomaster of Wittenberg. His circle included scholars, artists and the reformer Martin Luther, whose doctrine he adopted. Cranach was the leading artist of the Wittenberg Reformation, where he immortalised the movement's leaders in a series of portraits.

The Fall of the Rebel Angels 1554

Frans Floris 1519/20–1570
Panel, 308 x 220 cm
Central panel from the altarpiece
of the Swordsmen's Guild in
the Cathedral of Our Lady, Antwerp

and damaged as a result of the clash between the Catholic Church and Protestant reformers.

The theme comes from chapter 12 of St John's *Apocalypse* or *Book of Revelation*, the final book of the New Testament. In a fierce battle, the Archangel Michael and his angels drive away the crowned, seven-headed dragon and its monsters. The Archangel's forces are armed with swords (Michael was the patron saint of swordsmen), while the devil and his henchmen fight back with a knife, a mattock (a digging tool), a burning torch and a bow and arrow. Other elements from the vision of the Apocalypse appear in tiny scenes down the left edge: the Virgin on the crescent moon, clothed in the sun and a crown with twelve stars. She is menaced by the dragon, while her child is hurriedly led off to heaven. The incident highlights the ultimate defeat of the rebellious monster angels.

Frans Floris' biography is illustrative of the careers of many 16th-century artists in the Low Countries. As a young painter, he visited Italy, where he studied antique culture and contemporary art – the High Renaissance – in Rome and other Italian cities. Having returned to Antwerp, he successfully put his newly acquired skills into practice. Floris helped introduce mythological and allegorical themes to the Netherlands. His style is monumental and his figures are highly plastic in the manner of Michelangelo.

This panel was the centrepiece of a triptych that Frans Floris painted for the Swordsmen's Guild altar in Antwerp Cathedral. The wings probably disappeared during the Iconoclasm of 1566, when churches and abbeys were widely plundered

Market scenes crammed with fruit and vegetables, and peopled by market traders, growers and peasant women, began to appear in art around the mid-16th century. The genre is linked to the 'kitchen painting' and to the still life, and expressed the new spirit of the Renaissance and humanism, which brought a new focus on earthly reality, everyday life and nature. The 'reality' of this vegetable market is, however, relative. The produce displayed in the baskets and on the trays was never available all at the same time – cherries were picked in

40

ucts shown here were considered in the Middle Ages and beyond – in sermons and herbals alike – to have aphrodisiac properties, or else were used as amorous metaphors because of their shape or taste. The sweet taste of fruit, for instance, had long been compared in literature to the sweetness of lovemaking. In other words, all these erotic attributes tell a story – the old lady is going to pair off the pretty fruit-seller with the young fowler, clearly identified by the baskets of birds he has caught (the Dutch word 'vogelaar' meant both 'fowler' and 'womaniser'). We can guess what will happen next from the way the young people's hands approach one another and from the gaze of the procuress. Paintings like this were probably intended as a warning against immoral behaviour.

In addition to the ambiguous content, there is another intriguing aspect to works of this kind. The abundance of food radiates optimism. The suggestion is that Flanders was prospering in the second half of the 16th century, when it was, in fact, being tested by a bloody religious conflict and by social unrest.

The panel is signed and dated on the little wooden door in the background: JOCH BEUCKELAER 18 NOV.BRIS 1567. Joachim Beuckelaer, who ran a workshop in Antwerp, was a leading pioneer in the field of market and kitchen paintings, the popularity of which persisted far into the 17th century.

the early summer, medlars in the late autumn, raspberries in July, grapes in September, and so on. Nor, of course, would the display of goods in a real market have been quite so pristine.

In painting images like this, the artist was undoubtedly trying to show off his exceptional talent. Paintings always had a 'content' – preferably of a religious or moralising nature. Art historians began to explore this aspect of market paintings and related genres in the final quarter of the 20th century. They recognised that many of the prod-

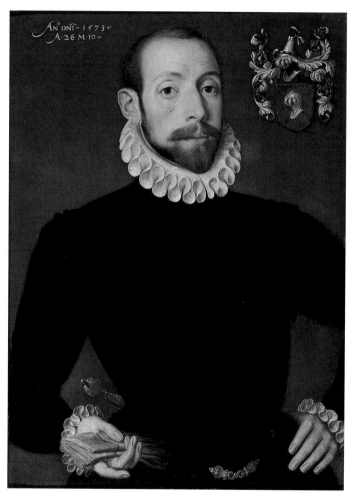

Anonymous, *Portrait of a Man*, 16th century.

the skilful observation with which the painter captured both the sitter's individuality and his social status. Some commentators view this late work as Pourbus' finest portrait.

Pieter Pourbus was the leading artist in Bruges in the second half of the 16th century and is sometimes referred to as the last of the Flemish Primitives. In addition to painting, he was a cartographer, surveyor and engineer. He is best known for his many outstanding individual and group portraits of the Bruges bourgeoisie.

It is interesting to compare this panel with two portraits from roughly the same period, which display a different style and an entirely different approach towards the model: the fluid *Portrait of a Man,* by an anonymous master, and the spontaneous *Portrait of a Young Man with a Letter* by an anonymous Dutch artist.

The nobleman Olivier van Nieulant poses formally for this official portrait. He was an alderman of Bruges, clerk of the court and council pensionary, and he wanted everybody to know it. Apart from his coat of arms, the painting includes his age and the date of the portrait. The image is sober but elegant, thanks to the position of the hands and certain costume details. It highlights

Topographical precision was the primary goal of the Antwerp painter Jacob Grimmer in his *View of the Kiel Estate*. The grandiose panoramic landscapes of artists like Joachim Patinir have given way here to a more realistic record. Grimmer liked to paint views of the area around Antwerp – in this case the former road to Hoboken, where the Kiel mansion once stood. In the distance on the right we make out the Antwerp skyline. The house is surrounded by a vegetable garden, orchard, pleasure garden, farm and several small houses. The painter has added a variety of picturesque touches to the landscape, including the little figures taking their leisure on the edges of the estate, and the colourful group of drunken, dancing and brawling fairgoers on the road. This cloudy, early evening landscape essentially illustrates the leisure pursuits of two contrasting social classes.

Pierson la Hues was drummer and messenger of Antwerp's Old Archery Guild. He is dressed in his guild uniform – ochre jerkin, red trunk-hose and stockings – and holds his black cap with its ostrich feather in his hand. He also wears his drum and his letter-pouch. A decorative chain runs across his chest, made up of silver plates that reflect his function. The top one has the figure of Fortuna, accompanied by the signature of the artist, *Gillis Congnet f.* (the spelling of his surname varied, with 'Congnet' and 'Coignet' occurring equally often). The inscription could also refer to the artist's father, who was a goldsmith and who may have produced the medal. The subtly characterised portrait in soft, yellowish brown with red tones reveals both the observational skills of the Antwerp painter and his familiarity with the painting style of the Venetian school. Coignet had, in fact, spent several years in Italy at the beginning of his career. He specialised in nocturnal scenes with chiaroscuro effects, in which he used gold to capture the glow of torches and candles. The lighting in this portrait is very subtle, especially the yellowish skin of the drum.

Pieter Brueghel the Younger
1564–1637/38
Panel, 41.5 x 58 cm

Pieter Brueghel the Younger was the eldest son of the famous Pieter Bruegel, by whom the museum has just one, very fine drawing (see p. 90). Around 1580, the Bruegel family moved from Brussels to Antwerp, where the sons Pieter and Jan trained as artists and became masters in their own right. Pieter worked in his father's style for the whole of his career. He painted countless copies and variations on Pieter the Elder's work, providing a useful service at a time when many of the originals were in private collections and could not be seen by the public. What is more, several of his father's paintings were lost, leaving only his son's faithful copies for posterity. This *Visit to the Farm* is a copy after a lost original by Pieter the Elder.

All manner of activity is going on in this farmhouse, centring on the fireplace with its cauldron of steaming porridge. The country people in the painting all appear well fed and the atmosphere is one of cheerful bustle. It is not clear precisely what is going on: the local landlord and his wife seem to be visiting one of their tenants following the birth of a child. There is certainly a mother sitting on a cradle near the fire with her baby on her lap. The gentleman is giving the tenant a present, while the lady is taking some money from her purse.

There are other, almost identical versions of the same composition by Pieter the Younger and also by his brother Jan, who painted the smaller copy that hangs nearby (1597). It is more refined than this one, but the mood is less lively because of his use of the grisaille technique in which the entire painting is executed in shades of a single colour – in this case brown.

a beautiful youth whom Jupiter decided to carry off to Mount Olympus to become cup-bearer to the gods. In return, he was granted immortality and eternal youth.

Paulus Bril was an Antwerp artist who travelled to Rome at the

Around the middle of the 16th century, artists influenced by the Italian Renaissance turned to classical mythology as a source of inspiration. Landscape painters now began to incorporate mythological scenes in their paintings, rather than biblical stories. This small panel is a good example. A horseman, a man on foot and three dogs stand watching in a broad landscape as Jupiter abducts Ganymede. According to classical mythology, Ganymede was

age of 20 and made his career there as a landscape specialist. He painted frescos in the Vatican and in Roman palaces. In addition to these monumental works, he also produced small oil paintings, often on copper. His work had a great deal of influence on later painters of 'Italianising' landscapes and seascapes.

46

St Luke Painting the Virgin's Portrait
1602

Marten de Vos 1531/32–1603
Panel, 270 x 217 cm
Central panel of the Painters' Guild altarpiece in the Cathedral of Our Lady, Antwerp

The open gospel on the right and the bull that kneels at St Luke's side are the saint's traditional attributes. The presence of the globe next to the table with the books gives the Renaissance interior the character of a humanist's study. Some historians have identified the figure of St Luke as a self-portrait of Marten de Vos. The apprentice, who is busy grinding pigments, is said in turn to be the painter Abraham Grapheus, by whom the museum has a portrait.

Like his teacher, Frans Floris, Marten de Vos spent several years in Italy, which is evident in his style and use of colour. Even so, his themes remained largely religious – he was one of the core of Antwerp painters responsible for refurbishing the city's churches after the iconoclastic destruction, which naturally imposed certain restrictions in terms of iconography.

The work is signed on the table leg on the far right: F.M.D. VOS 1602. Early paintings are often signed in odd places: anyone who takes the time to explore the signatures, dates, inscriptions and 'hidden' messages in the museum's old master collection is sure to make plenty of fascinating discoveries.

St Luke is the patron saint of painters, reflecting the early medieval legend that he had painted the Virgin Mary's portrait. Marten de Vos treats the theme here in a clear and balanced composition. The panel originally formed part of a triptych that decorated the Painters' Guild altar in Antwerp Cathedral. The wings, which were painted by other artists, have been lost.

Floral paintings became established as a pictorial genre in the Netherlands in the 16th century, reflecting the general humanist interest in nature, especially in botanical gardens. In the course of the century, a wide variety of scholarly herbals and botanical reference books – all accurately illustrated – were published in the Low Countries by authors like Dodoens, De Lobel and Clusius. The period ended with the appearance of the autonomous floral painting.

Jan Brueghel the Elder was one of the first flower painters. He developed a particularly luxuriant brand of floral arrangement, with which he was to enjoy immense success among his contemporaries.

The bouquet presented here, in a vase that presumably depicts the Four Elements (only Water and Earth are visible), is fantastical in several respects. In the first place, the flowers are rendered with amazing precision and are carefully arranged to show off their complex forms. It is as if this were less of a decorative bouquet than a deluxe catalogue of especially beautiful and, in those days, extremely expensive flowers. Above all, however, it is unreal in the sense that it is composed of flowers that normally bloom at different seasons (artificial cultivation did not exist in the early 17th century): tulips, peonies, lilies, roses and many others. The artist must, therefore, have composed his bouquet using botanical books and his own sketches and studies.

Joachim Beuckelaer adopted a similar procedure in his imaginary market scenes (see p. 40). In his case, the display of produce had a moralising purpose and in Jan Brueghel's floral paintings, too, there is more to discover than simply the breathtaking realism. Allegories were a crucial element in the art and literature of the day. Bringing together flowers from different seasons suggests the passing of time. Nature's annual cycle of budding, blooming and dying back conveys the idea of the transience of life.

Jan Brueghel the Elder, second son of Pieter Bruegel the Elder, was more talented and creative than his brother Pieter. He spent several years in Italy and subsequently became a much-admired artist in Antwerp and court painter to Archduke Albert and the Infanta Isabella. He specialised in floral pieces, still lifes and landscapes, to which he owed his nickname of 'Velvet Brueghel'. He frequently collaborated with artist friends, including Hendrik van Balen, Sebastiaan Vranckx, Joos de Momper and Peter Paul Rubens.

Helicon or *Minerva's Visit to the Muses* early 17th century	Joos II de Momper 1564–1635 Hendrik van Balen 1575–1632 Jan Brueghel the Elder 1568–1625 Panel, 140 x 199 cm

The painting illustrates the extent to which landscape art had evolved in the Netherlands in the century since Joachim Patinir. The background perspective has a lower viewpoint and the scene is less

The nine Muses perform a piece of music in the foreground, while the goddess Minerva approaches from the left. The scene is set on Helicon, a mountain in Greece devoted to the Muses. On the right, the winged horse Pegasus, with a blow of his hoof, causes the Hippocrene spring to gush forth.

Joos de Momper painted the landscape, Hendrik van Balen the figures and Jan 'Velvet' Brueghel the flowers. Their combined signature is inserted bottom right: BALE MOMPER BRUEGHEL. Works signed jointly by three artists are extremely rare.

panoramic than the Patinir-style 'world landscape' (see p. 32). The transition between foreground and background is more fluent. A broad, rolling valley opens up before us, rather than the wild, rocky outcrops that characterised the work of the artists' contemporary, Paulus Bril, in Italy (see p. 46). The mythological group is now a fully fledged component of the painting. The right-hand side of the foreground, with the spring, the waterfall and the trees, creates a shady frame through which we can view the landscape in the distance.

The Prodigal Son is shown begging for food in a corner, a mere detail in the overall painting, while a farm girl pours pig-feed into a trough. The religious theme is somewhat incidental. The New Testament story of the dissolute young man who falls into extreme poverty provided Rubens with the opportunity to paint one of his loveliest images of rural life. The painter focused in great detail on the stable, the farm equipment, the animals and the twilit landscape. The oxen have returned from the field, the horses shuffle impatiently and the farmhands of both sexes perform their final chores by candlelight. Like the many objects in the stable, the cart next to the farmhouse is painted from life with great precision. Powerful horizontals and verticals structure the composition. Diagonal perspective lines lead the eye into the distance, where a landscape with trees and two horses stretches out by a pond lit by the last rays of sunlight.

Rubens must have been especially fond of the work, as it remained in his possession until his death.

28 June 1577	P.P. Rubens is born in Siegen, Westphalia, on St Peter and St Paul's Day. His parents, the Antwerp lawyer Jan Rubens and Maria Pypelincx, had been forced to flee the Netherlands because of the war
1578	The family settles in Cologne
1589	Following the death of her husband, Maria Pypelincx returns to Antwerp with her children
1591–98	Peter Paul is apprenticed successively to Tobias Verhaecht, Adam van Noort and Otto van Veen
1598	Rubens enrols as a master painter in the Guild of St Luke
1600–08	Period in Italy as court painter to Duke Vincenzo Gonzaga. First-hand experience of the Italian Renaissance. Part of a diplomatic mission in 1603 to the Spanish court
1608	Rubens returns to Antwerp
1609	Appointed court painter to Archduke Albert and the Infanta Isabella, who grant him permission to remain in Antwerp and to work on his own account. Marries Isabella Brant
from 1609	Important commissions, including much religious work to refurbish churches damaged during the religious troubles. Affirmation of his baroque artistic vision
1613–15	Rockox triptych, *The Incredulity of St Thomas*
1614	*Venus Frigida*
c.1615	Builds a fine townhouse with a large workshop on Antwerp's Wapper
1618	*The Prodigal Son*
1617–20	Collaboration with Anthony van Dyck, including the decoration of Antwerp's Jesuit Church
from 1621	Following the death of Archduke Albert, Rubens becomes a political adviser to the Infanta Isabella until she too dies in 1633. Collects honours and titles in the Spanish Netherlands and abroad for his work as an artist and diplomat
1622–25	Maria de Medici commissions Rubens to decorate two galleries in the Palais de Luxembourg in Paris
1624	*Adoration of the Magi*
1626	Death of Isabella Brant
c.1628	Portrait of Gaspar Gevartius
1628–30	Diplomatic missions to Spain and London
1629–35	King Charles I of England commissions a series of paintings for the ceiling of the Banqueting House in Whitehall, London
1630	Rubens marries Hélène Fourment
1633	Appointed dean of the Guild of St Luke
1635	Purchases the country estate Het Steen, near Elewijt, where he spends his final summers
1636–38	King Philip IV of Spain commissions Rubens to decorate his hunting lodge, the Torre de la Parada
1638	*Triumphal Car of Kallo*
30 May 1640	Death of Peter Paul Rubens in Antwerp

Peter Paul Rubens was the most versatile and talented painter of the Flemish baroque. Together with Jacob Jordaens, Anthony van Dyck and many other masters, all of whom worked in his shadow, he helped establish Antwerp's artistic fame in the 17th century. He painted religious, historical, mythological and allegorical subjects, landscapes and portraits. He was also a talented draughtsman and designer of archi-

tectural features, tapestries and book illustrations. His work is marked by its *joie de vivre* and powerful sense of nature, both of which were expressed in an elegant, sensual style and a rich palette. The museum has 21 paintings and oil sketches by Rubens.

Rubens was famous for his mythological paintings: *Venus Frigida* (1614) is a good example of the genre. The artist was inspired by a classical marble statue of Venus that he saw in Rome, which he used to illustrate a quotation from the Roman playwright Terence: 'Sine Cerere et Libero friget Venus' (roughly, 'hunger and thirst cool the flames of love').

The Incredulity of St Thomas 1613–15   Peter Paul Rubens 1577–1640
Panel, 143 x 123 cm (central panel),
146 x 55 cm (wings)
Memorial triptych of Nicolaas Rockox
and Adriana Perez in Antwerp's
Franciscan Church

Rubens painted this triptych for his friend Nicolaas Rockox (1560–1640), burgomaster of Antwerp. The patron is shown in the left wing, while his wife, Adriana Perez (?–1619), appears on the right. The painting was intended for their eventual tomb in a chapel in the city's Franciscan Church.

The Incredulity of St Thomas illustrates the incident in the New Testament when the resurrected Christ appears to his disciples and shows them the wounds in his hands to prove that he really has risen from the dead. It was an appropriate subject for a memorial chapel.

The triptych dates from Rubens' 'classical' period between 1612 and 1615, the characteristic features of which were the calm, uncluttered style, the restrained poses, the even lighting, without heavy shadows, and the silvery sheen of the colours. The figures in these compositions are often shown half-length.

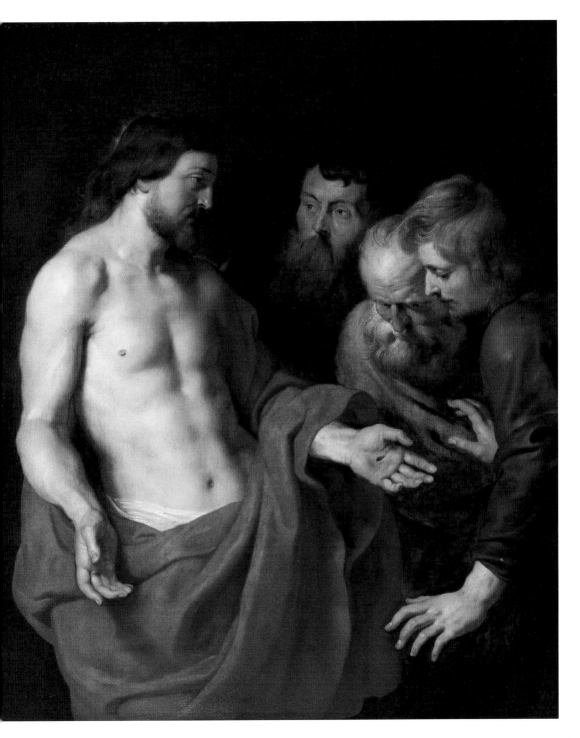

The Adoration of the Magi 1624

Peter Paul Rubens 1577–1640
Panel, 447 x 336 cm
Altarpiece from the high altar
of Antwerp's Abbey of St Michael

The Adoration of the Magi is one of Rubens' loveliest altarpieces and a triumphal exemplar of the high baroque. The work stands out for its lively, asymmetrical composition, the richly nuanced colours, the fluency of the painting and the expressiveness of the figures. The highly varied and turbulent group is held together by several robust vertical elements in the architecture, a horizontal beam at the top and several diagonal beams that run parallel to the main lines of the composition. The monumental panel is also exceptional in technical terms: in certain areas, Rubens limits himself to a few broad brushstrokes with which to create forms that stand out against the light ochre layer beneath, as we see in the lower right zone with the cow's head and the straw on the floor. What Rubens is actually doing is to apply the technique of the oil sketch on a larger scale: tradition has it that he completed the painting in two weeks. The brilliant, precise touch and the sparing use of paint suggest that the story may well be true.

The altarpiece originally belonged to the once powerful Abbey of St Michael, which was closed at the beginning of the 19th century.

Portrait of Gaspar Gevartius c.1628   Peter Paul Rubens 1577–1640
Panel, 119 x 98 cm

In addition to his many commissions for the Church, Rubens also painted non-religious works for royalty, nobles and prominent burghers. There was plenty of demand, as many leading contemporaries were keen to have him paint their portraits. Gaspar Gevartius was Antwerp's municipal clerk, hence the pen and record book on his writing table. The marble bust in the background is that of the Roman philosopher-emperor Marcus Aurelius, whose works Gevartius studied and annotated. The image is basically limited to the triangle formed above the diagonal running from the lower left to the upper right corner. The black jerkin and the dark background, and the white millstone collar and pages, focus the viewer's attention on the face and on the movement of the hands.

The sitter was a close friend of Rubens – a personal bond that is suggested by Gevartius' relaxed pose, as if he were looking up from his work to speak to the artist as he dropped in for a visit.

In 1638, the Spanish governor of the Southern Netherlands, the Cardinal-Infante Don Ferdinand, defeated the Dutch at Kallo, near Antwerp, and the French at Saint-Omer (in French Flanders). Antwerp's civic authorities decided to celebrate these victories and commissioned Rubens to design a triumphal carriage. It is conceived as a ship with all manner of allegorical female figures, including Prosperity, Providence, Courage and personifications of Antwerp and Saint-Omer. On a pedestal in the middle, we see Victory as two winged virgins with garlands of flowers and an inscribed medallion. This rapidly executed oil sketch testifies to the deftness of Rubens' painting style.

jealous companions are angry and the ensuing quarrel will eventually cost Meleager his life.

Unlike his contemporaries, Rubens and Van Dyck, Jacob Jordaens never visited Italy. Even so, he was influenced by Italian art at the beginning of his career, especially Caravaggio's treatment of light.

The Caravaggesque chiaroscuro is even stronger in another early work, the *Adoration of the Shepherds* (c. 1616), in which a candle and a lantern are the only sources of light. All trace of this Italian influence disappeared within the space of a few years, when Jordaens – like virtually all his colleagues – adopted Rubens' style.

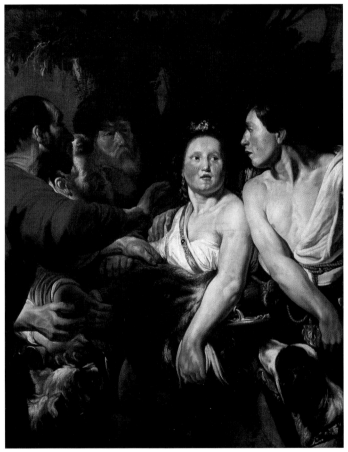

In his *Metamorphoses*, Ovid tells the story of Meleager, son of the King of Calydon, who kills a giant, destructive wild boar and presents the head and skin to the girl Atalanta, with whom he has fallen in love. Jordaens shows the moment when Atalanta receives the boar's head. It is a dramatic episode, as Meleager's

This is plain in *Meleager and Atalanta*, where the contrasts between light and shadow accentuate the emotionally charged moment. Atalanta looks at Meleager anxiously, as he reaches for his sword in response to the men's protests. The two lovers are brightly lit against an impenetrably dark background. We also sense the coming disaster from the men's threatening hand movements.

Six people from three generations sit around a table set for a meal. The old man sings as he beats time with one hand and holds a songbook in the other; the old lady opposite him is also singing. The younger generation play wind instruments: the toddler on its mother's lap plays a toy whistle, the other child a recorder and the man at the back a bagpipe. The young mother sits in the middle of this family group, listening with pleasure to the music.

The words in the cartouche at

the top read 'Soo d'oude songen, soo pepen de jonge' ('as the old sang, so the young twitter'). In other words, the young follow their elders' example. The proverb comes from the collected wisdom of Jacob Cats, *Spiegel Van den Ouden ende Nieuwen Tijdt* (1632). The painter appears to have used a different version at first, as the inscription has clearly been corrected and over-painted.

The theme must have been a favourite of Jordaens and his customers, as he painted many versions of it, sometimes with the help of his workshop assistants. This painting is the earliest known example and shows the artist at his best.

Jacob Jordaens is considered to be one of the greatest Flemish masters of the baroque. He worked for his whole life in Antwerp, where he headed an important workshop. Although he was a versatile painter, his artistic aspirations were not as high as those of Rubens or Van Dyck. The character that comes over from his paintings is that of a straightforward burgher with little interest in sublime emotion or philosophical reflection. His style is characterised by its vigorous touch and the thick application of paint. His figures are usually pressed together, they radiate *joie de vivre* and sensuality, and are bathed in a marvellous warm light. The deaths of Rubens in 1640 and Van Dyck in 1641 made Jordaens the leading painter in the Southern Netherlands.

This portrait of a man in a black jerkin and a fine lace collar shows the Antwerp painter Marten Pepijn. As noted on the right of the panel, he was 58 years old at the time. The painting must have been executed in the first few months of 1632 as Van Dyck moved to London at the beginning of April.

Marten Pepijn is presented very simply, dressed in unassuming black clothes and set against a brown background, yet the lack of ostentation simply makes his spirited face seem all the more impressive. His gleaming forehead, thinning salt-and-pepper hair, unruly beard and lively gaze are painted sensitively and fluently.

The painting was subsequently enlarged. The joins are visible on all four sides, as we see, for example, just above Van Dyck's signature.

As a young artist, **Anthony van Dyck** spent some time working with Rubens. He then left his native Antwerp for several years to visit Italy and England. Van Dyck was strongly influenced by the Venetian painter Titian who, together with Rubens, was to remain his greatest source of inspiration. In 1632, King Charles I invited him to London, where he remained until his death. Van Dyck was appointed court painter and went on to enjoy immense prestige. Although he also painted religious and mythological scenes, he was best known for his portraits of the haute bourgeoisie and nobility of Genoa, Antwerp and London. He immortalised the glittering court of Charles I shortly before its downfall during the English Civil War.

Van Dyck produced this *Lamentation* during a brief visit to Flanders in 1634–35 for the former diplomat Abbé Cesare Alesandro Scaglia. He painted an impressive portrait of Scaglia, which also belongs to the museum, during the same visit.

The *Lamentation* was intended for the church of Antwerp's Franciscan Abbey, where the Abbé intended to spend the final years of his life. The iconographical theme of the Lamentation presents the moment when those who had been closest to Christ during his life have gathered around his dead body, which has just been lowered from the Cross. The emphatically horizontal shape of the canvas – it probably functioned as the predella of a large altarpiece – obliged Van Dyck to spread the composition across the field of view. The body rests in the Virgin Mary's lap in the custom-ary way, but the artist positions the figures closer to the ground. Similarly, he makes Mary lean back a little and the other figures lean forward, while the pale, elongated body of Christ runs across the composition like a long, low diagonal. Mary's open arms close off the composition on the left and draw in the two grieving angels on the right. St John gently raises Jesus' left arm and points to the nail wound in the hand.

Van Dyck's strong sense of monumentality and drama are clearly displayed in this painting. His rendering of the impotent grief of a mother who has lost her son gives the work a universal dimension.

The wealthy merchant Sebastiaan Leerse sits proudly with his wife and young son in their 'constkamer' – the room in which he kept his private collection of paintings and classical (some of it pseudo-classical) sculpture. The bouquet on the table recalls the floral paintings of Jan 'Velvet' Brueghel. The chamber also contains several of the exotic pets that were fashionable at the time – the little monkey sitting on the floor and the two parrots on their perch. Similar creatures appear frequently in the still lifes and pantries that Frans Snyders painted (see p. 68).

In this painting, Frans Francken the Younger combines two genres that were very popular in 17th-century Antwerp – family portraits and art galleries. Many wealthy townspeople of that era had their own private galleries, some larger than others. Rubens, for instance, owned many paintings and collector's items like coins and classical sculpture. Paintings of these galleries are very interesting as historical documents, in that they provide a glimpse – albeit an artificially lavish one – of the interiors and art collections of 17th-century Antwerp. Surprisingly, it is a theme that occurs almost exclusively in Flemish art.

Francken launched the 'constkamer' as an autonomous pictorial genre and made it his speciality. He signed the painting in an interesting place – on the canvas of *Apelles Painting the Beautiful Campaspe* that leans against the chair in the bottom right corner. No such painting by him is known, although it may have been lost over the years. On the other hand, the reference to Alexander the Great's mythical court painter could be pure invention, intended as a tribute to Mevrouw Leerse.

This popular scene is a typical 'genre painting'. The term is used to describe scenes from everyday life or illustrations of people's morals and customs, possibly with a humorous or moralising undertone. Genre works first became an autonomous strand in Netherlandish painting in the 16th century but the theme was to reach its peak in the 17th century and in the Northern Netherlands, with artists like Jan Steen, Adriaan van Ostade, Pieter de Hooch, Johannes Vermeer and others. The Antwerp painters Adriaan Brouwer and David Teniers the Younger were also leading exponents of genre painting.

Adriaan Brouwer drew his themes exclusively from peasant life. Shabby villagers sit in miserable taverns, drinking, smoking, playing cards or brawling. This small panel, with its marvellous, velvety colours, is no exception, highlighting as it does the undesirable behaviour of the 'common people'. Images of this kind were intended to entertain and to edify respectable townspeople, who liked to think that they lived by different standards. The poodle is an odd feature in such surroundings and probably had some special significance.

Having trained in Haarlem and Amsterdam, the Fleming Adriaan Brouwer settled in Antwerp. His palette was virtually monochrome, with finely nuanced brown and green shades and the occasional colourful accent. *Card Players and Drinkers* illustrates both this subtle form of colour composition and Brouwer's mercilessly satirical view of poor people's lives.

David Teniers mainly painted ordinary people but his attitude towards peasant life is friendlier and more idealised than Adriaan Brouwer's. This early work shows a 'smoking den' – a musty chamber in which a group of young people sit smoking. The tobacco is mixed, the pipe lit and the smoke inhaled with relish. Tobacco was introduced to Europe from overseas only in the second half of the 16th century. By the beginning of the 17th, pipe-smoking – a habit spread by seamen and soldiers – had become a passion among all layers of society. Moral guardians warned against it, as they did against drinking, dancing and other supposedly pernicious sensual pleasures. In this case, the artist is warning the viewer. The sputtering candle by the wall is an allusion to the fleeting enjoyment to be had from such addictive pastimes. Attitudes started to change around the end of the 17th century. Smoking began to be used in images of the Five Senses to represent the sense of smell, and tobacco was even ascribed medicinal properties.

In addition to genre paintings, the other important strand in Teniers' art was the landscape, examples of which can also be seen in the museum.

Portrait of a Small Boy 17th century

Erasmus Quellin 1607–1678
Jan Fijt (animals) 1611–1661
Panel, 136 x 103 cm

A small child stands before a landscape, with the Antwerp skyline in the distance. It is a little boy, although that is not immediately obvious. The dress and white bonnet he wears are typical of the 17th century, and he is equipped for falconry, with the bird itself, the accompanying bag, glove and hood, a feathered hat, a greyhound and a hunting dog. The little hunter-to-be is probably the son of an aristocratic family.

The animals were painted by Jan Fijt who, like Erasmus Quellin, worked in Antwerp. Collaboration of this kind between artists was fairly common in Flanders, reflecting the degree of specialisation.

In addition to still lifes and market and kitchen paintings, pantries also emerged as an artistic theme towards the end of the 16th century. The Antwerp painter Frans Snyders brought the genre to its peak in the 17th century.

Like Joachim Beuckelaer in the 16th century and Jan Brueghel the Elder at the beginning of the 17th, Snyders inserted a hidden message in his lavish displays of natural produce. A well-stocked larder suggests the properly run household of a wealthy townsman or landowner in peacetime and so, in this sense, the theme may be interpreted as a plea for peace. The population of the Southern Netherlands had, after all, been subjected to almost continuous war for almost a hundred years. Abundance like this also praises the beauty and usefulness of God's creation, and may even allude to the popular expression 'alles met mate' (everything in moderation).

The enticing array of food in this pantry is disturbed, however, by several impudent household animals – a parrot pecks at the grapes, a monkey filches a little basket of hazelnuts and a small, growling dog appears from beneath the table. The dog is supposed to be guarding the pantry, but has clearly failed in its duty. The atmosphere is one of disorder and uncontrolled urges. Frans Snyders presents us with a moral lesson, although it is impossible now to say whether it concerns statecraft or family life. Moderation,

Snyders' paintings are realistic and colourful, with a strongly tactile feel and refined light effects.

reason, order and vigilance are all recommended by showing us their opposite.

The Easterlings' House in Antwerp
first half 17th century

Lucas van Uden 1595–1672
Panel, 41 x 71 cm

Lucas van Uden devoted himself entirely to landscape painting. Although he is one of the less inspired masters of the 17th-century Antwerp school, his paintings still have a great deal of atmosphere and are executed with great technical care. This winter view with ice-skaters in the distance shows the house in Antwerp that was once occupied by the 'Easterlings' or Hanseatics – merchants from Northern and Western Germany. The Hanseatics' house was built on the outskirts of the city, in a new district called 'Nieuwstad' (New Town), which explains the large open space in front of the building.

The Hansa and its merchants had long since left the city by the time Lucas van Uden painted the building with its imposing tower. At the time of the painting, it was used for storage, before subsequently being demolished altogether.

The diversity of Flemish landscape art in the 17th century is plain if we compare Joos de Momper's mythological scene (p. 50), Lucas van Uden's topographical image and the rustic view in the background of Rubens' *Prodigal Son* with this little patch of nature, in which a couple of women, presented from a low viewpoint, are going about their everyday business. The impressionistic atmosphere and the idealised, rural simplicity are the most appealing elements in Siberechts' work, which seems to evoke Arcadia in the countryside around 17th-century Antwerp.

*Portrait of Stefanus Geraerdts c.*1651

Frans Hals c. 1582–1666
Canvas, 115 x 87 cm
Wedding portrait: the pendant
portrait of Isabella Coymans is in
a private collection in Paris

Stefanus Geraerdts' clothes are brilliantly
rendered in black, white and gold brushstrokes.

A cheerful Stefanus Geraerdts looks
at his wife, Isabella Coymans, who
presents him with a rose. It is clear
from his clothes that he is a member
of Dutch high society: his plump
figure and the smile on his moon-
shaped face positively radiate prosperity. This image of a happy couple
is one of the most attractive and
original of Frans Hals' paintings. It is
a great shame that the pair of portraits was separated, breaking the
eye contact between the two figures.

Frans Hals left his native Amsterdam as a child and settled in Haarlem. He probably trained under the painter
Karel van Mander before enrolling in Haarlem's Guild of St Luke in 1610. Hals is famous for his genre paintings and portraits, which he produced with a loose technique all of his own. His models – whether ordinary
people or Haarlem worthies – are never rendered stereotypically or harshly, but with incomparable vivacity
and realism. His militia paintings – 'official' group portraits of militia members – are unconventional and
dynamic compositions. Since his rediscovery in the 19th century, Hals has been viewed as one of the greatest
portrait painters of all time.

Gerard Terborch belongs to the group of 17th-century Dutch masters who have won eternal fame with their still lifes, portraits, landscapes and genre paintings. He worked for most of his life in Zwolle and Deventer, where he concentrated on portraits and genre paintings. His interiors and their bourgeois occupants, who often play musical instruments, radiate prestige and intimacy. His use of colour is sober and subtle, his compositions are simple and clearly conceived, and he differentiates brilliantly between materials and fabrics. Above all, he was a masterful and sensitive interpreter of human behaviour.

It is often said that his genre paintings contain concealed morals or dual meanings. This one is supposedly about love, with the lute as a symbol of romantic harmony – its charming tones expressive of sweet emotions – 'amor docet musicam' (music is taught by love), as a 17th-century book of proverbs had it.

The lute player herself is Gerard Terborch's sister Gesina, whom he often used as a model. The painter's signature appears on the spine of the book lying on the table with the Turkish rug: *G t Borg fct.*

Floris Gerritzoon van Schooten, *Breakfast,*
first half 17th century.

The glittering still lifes of the Dutch painter Abraham van Beyeren are among the best the genre has to offer. He painted theatrical arrangements with draped tablecloths, silver platters and sparkling Venetian glassware, in which an abundance of fruit and other food is brought together, probably with a symbolic undertone. Peeled lemons and crabs are among his most frequent motifs and both may have had some emblematic meaning. Still lifes are indirect reminders of the transience of all earthly beauty and pleasure and they implicitly admonish the viewer to show moderation. This moral message was by no means, however, the painter's main concern.

Apart from still lifes with fruit, there were sober, though no less refined, 'breakfasts' and selections of confectionery. The museum has a fine example of a Dutch *Breakfast* by Floris Gerritzoon van Schooten (first half 17th century).

Samuel van Hoogstraeten, a 17th-century art theorist, wrote in his *Inleyding tot de Hooge Schoole der Schilderkonst* (Introduction to the High School of Painting): 'A perfect painting is like a mirror to nature, which makes things that do not exist seem like they do.' That is precisely what 17th-century still life painters set out to do with their deceptive realism.

Vanitas second half 17th century

Franciscus Gysbrechts
second half 17th century
Canvas, 115 x 134 cm

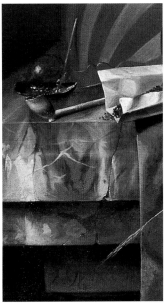

Objects alluding to a variety of human activities are arranged around a skull – it is hard to imagine a more explicit image of the transience of human existence. The artist highlights the vanity of intellectual pursuits (books, documents and the globe) and of pleasure (musical instruments and score, pipe and tobacco). The hourglass reminds us of the passing of time and the bubbles of the fragility of life, while the snuffed-out candle and the skull, wreathed in cornstalks, refer to the fate that no human being can escape.

Still lifes of this kind are known as 'vanitas' images, after the phrase from *Ecclesiastes*: 'Vanitas vanita-

tum, omnia vanitas' (Vanity of vanities, and everything is vanity). The genre was very popular in the 17th century.

Little is known about the Leiden painter Franciscus Gysbrechts. Only a small number of works by him are known, most of which are mysterious, richly embellished vanitas paintings like this one.

table. The tea caddy and several cups stand ready, while a woman bends over a small stove on which the kettle is heating. A little girl with a cup of tea sits in the right foreground.

Tea was introduced into Europe from the Far East only around the middle of the 17th century. By the end of the century, however, it had become the favourite drink of the nobility and bourgeoisie, who organised intimate gatherings around the tea-making ritual. The scene that Horemans presents here is undoubtedly ambiguous: the frivolous painting above the fireplace and the plucked chicken and sausages hanging from the ceiling reveal the sensual undertone.

When it came to decorating their homes, bourgeois patrons in the 18th century retained their taste for portraits, still lifes, landscapes and scenes from everyday life. Many artists continued to work with traditional themes. Jan Jozef Horemans the Younger, for instance, drew inspiration from 17th-century genre paintings for charming works like *Tea Time* and *The Card Game*.

Tea Time shows an interior with a lively group of people around a

Portrait of the Artist A.C. Lens c. 1770   Willem J. Herreyns 1743–1827
Canvas, 116 x 96 cm

The neo-classical painter Andries Cornelis Lens poses in his studio surrounded by the attributes of his profession: plastercasts of classical sculptures, palette, paintbrushes, a painting, preparatory sketches and books. His self-conscious, theatrical pose and the baroque drapery of his cloak reflect the tradition of the 17th-century court portrait. Lens was a prestigious artist, court painter to Charles of Lorraine, governor of the Austrian Netherlands in Brussels.

Willem Herreyns also sought to achieve greater psychological depth – a new development in portrait painting. Herreyns and Lens both came from Antwerp and were friends. Each served at different times as principal of Antwerp's Academy of Fine Art.

Storm at Sea second half 18th century   Jan Baptist Tency 18th century
                                          Panel, 52 x 79 cm

Claude Joseph Vernet, *Seascape*,
second half 18th century.

A sailing ship capsizes in a fierce storm. Members of its crew try to reach the shore, while onlookers stand on the rocks, gesticulating and seeking to help. Some distance away, another ship navigates with great difficulty into the entrance of the harbour.

This is the only authenticated work by Jan Baptist Tency in a museum collection. Tency appears to have come from Brussels, but we know virtually nothing about his life.

It is not only the swirling sea, the threatening clouds and the flashes of lightning that lend this scene its powerful drama. The dark rocks that border it on either side, the bushes that stand out against the sky and the tiny figures all contribute to the seascape's romantic and overwhelming effect.

Tency's work is related to that of the French painter Joseph Vernet (1714–1789). The museum has a typical Vernet seascape, in which we find a similar combination of savage waves, human drama and picturesque detail.

The Romantic movement reached its peak in Europe between the end of the 18th century and the middle of the 19th. An urgent desire for free expression arose in both literature and art, as a reaction to the strait-jacket of rationalism and classicism. Artists began to pursue new values like imagination, emotion, nature, patriotism, individualism and a sense of history. The specific accents differed from one country to another, according to the national temperament.

In Belgium, which had become an independent monarchy in 1830, there was a powerful focus on the national past and on the struggle for liberty. Gustaf Wappers was the leading Romantic painter in this respect. He worked primarily in Antwerp, where he was principal of the Academy for many years, and in Paris.

He creates a powerful sense of dramatic tension in *The De Witt Brothers in Captivity*. The simplicity of the composition enhances its elo-quence. Cornelis and Johan de Witt were statesmen who were impris-oned in 1672 for opposing the House of Orange. They were dragged from their cell and murdered by an angry mob. In the painting, they seem to be listening anxiously to the cries of the approaching crowd.

This panel recalls an important moment in Belgium's cultural past, when the German artist and draughtsman Albrecht Dürer travelled through the Netherlands in 1520–21. Dürer was a real celebrity and was received with great cere-

mony in all the cities he visited. He chose Antwerp as his temporary base, where he met a variety of contemporary artists including Quentin Massys and Joachim Patinir. His time in the Low Countries was immensely important both to Dürer himself and to local artists.

Like Gustaf Wappers, Henri Leys was a Belgian Romantic painter, yet he chose an entirely dif-

ferent path. Rather than the baroque and heroic images we find in Wappers' works, Leys looked to the tradition of the 17th-century genre painting, preferring to depict scenes of everyday life in the 16th century. He did so with documen-

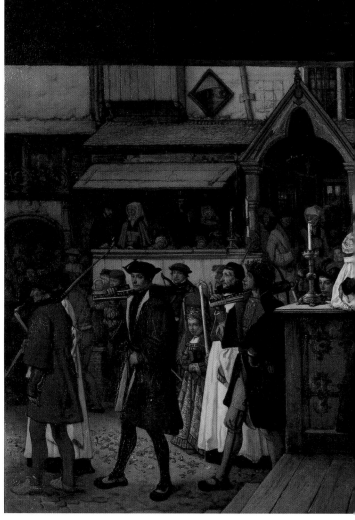

tary precision and a lack of sentimentality, in a style that recalls that of the Flemish Primitives and German Renaissance painters. His paintings offer a crisp reconstruction of the past. Like the early Flemish masters, he preferred to paint on wooden panels using gleaming, saturated colours and clearly outlined forms. There is an element of distance and nostalgia in his historical realism.

The world of Parisian women, with their elegant appearance, glamorous friends and complex love lives, was the favoured theme of the Brussels painter Alfred Stevens, who settled in the French capital as a young artist. He began by painting realistic and socially engaged works, but from the 1860s onwards he concentrated almost exclusively on 'praising the modern woman', especially those belonging to the Parisian *demi-monde*. His best work includes this *Parisian Sphinx* – an enigmatic portrait that eschews expensive trinkets and the details of a bourgeois interior and concentrates instead on immortalising the subtly lit and rather impatient-looking model.

The Josaphat Valley in Schaarbeek 1868 Hippolyte Boulenger 1837–1874
Panel, 110 x 85 cm

The pictorial technique and natural
colouring of this work are typical of
the innovative art of Hippolyte
Boulenger. Nature is rendered realistically, yet with plenty of atmosphere and interesting lighting
effects.

Boulenger came from Tournai
and played an important part in the
development of landscape art in
Belgium. Following the example of
the Romantic-Realist painters of the
French Barbizon school, he worked
in the open air and sought to
achieve a more intense contact with
nature. He was able in this way to
break with the tradition of the composed, academic landscape. He preferred to paint locations around
Brussels and in the Ardennes, and
became the leading figure in the
'Tervuren School', which brought
together a number of *plein-air*
artists around Boulenger's home
just outside Brussels. His style gradually became less realistic and he
began to practise a kind of dark
Impressionism.

Henri de Braekeleer spent his entire life in Antwerp. He was born in the city on 11 June 1840 and died there on 20 July 1888. Two artists had a major influence on his formative years: his father Ferdinand, who was a respected genre and history painter, and his uncle, Henri Leys, who was an internationally known painter of historical genre scenes (see p. 80). His two relatives had a greater impact on Henri's work than the Antwerp Academy, where De Braekeleer studied as a young man between 1854 and 1861.

His only noteworthy trip outside Antwerp occurred in 1863–64, when he travelled to Germany and the Netherlands to collect study material for Henri Leys. In Amsterdam he admired the works of the 17th-century Dutch genre painters, especially Pieter de Hooch and Johannes Vermeer, and his interest grew as the years passed. De Braekeleer never married and continued to live with his parents. His favourite model was his sister Betsy.

He started out with a minutely realistic and anecdotal style (*Flower Grower's Garden*) but the sense of physicality and detail came gradually to be associated with a looser technique and an impressionistic sense of light and atmosphere. His interiors, with their daydreaming or absorbed occupants, are filled with a nostalgic and sometimes oppressive stillness (*Man in a Chair*). An open window looking out at the old city of Antwerp fails to break the sense of enclosure. In the later part of his career, De Braekeleer often painted in small, quivering strokes that produce a shimmering light in his overstuffed interiors *(The Meal)*. The supple brushwork of his landscapes and beach views gives them a fresh and informal feel.

Around 1880 De Braekeleer suffered a physical and mental breakdown, from which he recovered slowly; thereafter he worked much less than he once had. The still lifes he painted in this period display a modern, free style and a vivid palette.

Henri de Braekeleer was the leading Flemish painter of the 19th century before the appearance of James Ensor. The museum has 33 of his paintings and 45 watercolours and drawings.

It is plain from 'its realistic character', as a contemporary critic put it, that this is an early De Braekeleer. The artistic journals of the time were scornful of the style and the popular subject matter, which they described as 'banal genre' and 'realistic folly'. The painting is nowadays viewed as the artist's first important work. He was 24 at the time and freshly returned from a visit to Amsterdam, where he had been impressed by 17th-century Dutch masters like Steen, Metsu, Vermeer and De Hooch.

The photographic crispness and detail of this flower grower's garden, probably near to his parents' house on Antwerp's Mechelsesteenweg, have a poetic feel. It was a poetry, moreover, that was to intensify in his subsequent work as the artist's personal feelings began to push out the anecdotal element. In spite of its realism, there is something unnatural about the painting. The perfect rows of pots, plants and cold frames, and the minute record of every roof tile, stone and leaf do not belong to the real, ever-changing world. Only the clouds seem to have any movement – all the rest is frozen.

You could be forgiven for thinking that the gold leather wall covering was the main theme of this painting. The interiors of wealthy Flemish burghers were dressed with gold leather in the 16th, 17th and 18th centuries. Examples of authentic 16th-century gold leather wall hangings can be seen today in the Plantin-Moretus Museum.

It is hard to say whether the unmistakable sadness that emanates from this painting comes from the open, viewless window or the deeply melancholy expression of the man staring so listlessly. A former chief curator of the museum once wrote: 'The man's heart is filled with an inexpressible grief. What should he care about the miraculous light that fills the room?' De Braekeleer was fond of old Antwerp interiors and liked to paint rich and varied textures. What most interested him about this room in the Brouwershuis was the marvellous gold leather wall covering. The man in the chair seems totally overwhelmed by it all.

A contemporary of the artist recalled that he had no fixed studio as he did not want to work in the same light all the time. He visited a variety of interiors and, if the lighting and the location appealed to him, he set up there for a while and produced two or three paintings. Nevertheless, this impressionistic interior, so rich in atmosphere and nuances of light, painted so precisely and yet so fluently, is first and foremost a meditation on human beings as solitary and mortal.

In an overstuffed interior, several exquisite still lifes are grouped around the woman at the table. This is not the real dining room of the De Braekeleer family – the artist has not simply captured his sister Betsy on canvas at an unguarded moment. What we see is a stage set. Although middle-class homes really were crammed full in those days, the total lack of room in which to manoeuvre is not realistic. The artist clearly enjoyed painting all kinds of fabrics and materials, across which the light spreads in an infinity of nuances. He painted the same room in other works (includ-

ing *The Card Players*, in the Musées Royaux des Beaux-Arts in Brussels), with different though equally busy furnishings.

Even so, this scene has the appearance of real life, with Betsy stuffing a segment of orange into her mouth. Attentive viewers will notice, however, that her seemingly spontaneous pose is echoed in the small painting on the wall. The painter seems to be telling us that we do not see what we think we see – painting is merely appearance.

A trio of colliery workers – two men and a woman – walk along a path that runs high above the workers' houses, slag heaps, coalmines and smoking chimneys. The heavy work of the day is over and they are going home. Constantin Meunier has given the three monumental figures – especially the man in the middle – an air of dignity and self-assurance.

Meunier was aged about 50 when he discovered the world of the Walloon metal and coal industry, which prompted him to devote himself wholeheartedly to the theme of the worker. He was a sculptor and painter who created masterpieces in both forms, in which he glorified the strength and nobility of the working man – the leading actor in an epic tale of hard labour.

Like Constantin Meunier, the Brussels jeweller's son Léon Frederic was struck by the living conditions of the working class. He expressed his social engagement through realistic, sharply outlined images of industrial and agricultural workers. He was introduced to the poverty of the Walloon countryside during a stay in the Ardennes. This portrait of two Walloon peasant girls dates from that period.

Frederic liked to paint grandiloquent, allegorical themes, which he conceived as polyptychs or series. *Two Walloon Peasant Girls* is an exception, the simplicity of which makes it so moving. The flaking wall above the simple wooden panelling is powerfully suggestive. All our attention is focused on the two young sisters, with no symbolism, no hidden meanings and no superfluous details. The children's penetrating gaze follows you, wherever you stand. The artist achieved this effect with a technique used by 18th-century portraitists.

Pieter Bruegel the Elder, *Landscape with Three Pilgrims*, c. 1555,
pen and brown ink, (later) brown wash, 26 x 41.5 cm.

Pieter Bruegel travelled to Italy between 1551 and 1554/55. He was deeply
impressed by the natural beauty he encountered *en route* and, having returned
to Antwerp, he drew a series of large landscapes that recall his journey over the
Alps. They were published as a collection of twelve prints by the Antwerp
engraver Hieronymus Cock. This image with its three pilgrims was a design for
the print *The Men of Emmaus*.

The museum has a collection of around 3,600 drawings and prints, mostly from the 19th and 20th centuries, although there are several valuable items from earlier periods, including the pen-and-ink drawing *Landscape with Three Pilgrims* by Pieter Bruegel the Elder (*c.* 1525–1569). The most important groups of drawings in the collection are by the following artists (all figures approximate): Nicaise de Keyser (850), James Ensor (over 600), Henri de Braekeleer (40), William A. Sherwood (100), Jakob Smits (40), Jan Antoon Verschaeren (100), Willem Paerels (40), Rik Wouters (65) and Paul Joostens (170).

James Ensor, *The Cuirassiers at Waterloo*, 1891, pastel and Indian ink, 22.5 x 62.5 cm.

Between 1889 and 1892, Ensor produced a series of drawings about Napoleon's defeat at Waterloo. This sheet – which actually consists of three leaves of paper pasted onto cardboard – illustrates the moment at which some 10,000 French cavalrymen (cuirassiers) boxed in the British infantry. Left: the surrounded British infantry with their officers on horseback in the middle. Right: the French cuirassiers. Far right, top: the British cavalry. The drawing offers an expansive panorama in miniature, with brilliant colour, line and atmosphere.

At the beginning of his artistic career, at the age of about 20, Ensor began to paint figures in bourgeois interiors, mostly relatives in the salon or drawing room of his parents' house in Ostend. He used a dark palette, in which the limited amount of light entering the room plays an important role. The highly expressive and sensitive use of paint, with colours that blend and vibrate, and the uninhibited brushwork were revolutionary in Belgian art at the time.

In each of these works, Ensor provides us with a moment in the life of the provincial bourgeoisie. In this example we see one woman sewing and another reading. The curtains are half-drawn, seemingly closing the room off from the light of the sun and the noises of the street. The atmosphere is somewhat oppressive. The artist, who observes the room from a fairly high viewpoint, introduces a note of tension and confusion into this tranquil little world. Vigorously brushed masses of paint blur the contour lines, the carpeted floor becomes unstable and objects are assailed by the light that Ensor seized on and made his own.

It was not long before Ensor adopted a lighter palette and a more modern approach, influenced by the Impressionists and, above all, by J.M.W. Turner. It was too advanced for many of his contemporaries, and several exhibition committees rejected *Woman Eating Oysters*. The painting was not shown in public until 1886, when it was accepted for the salon of the progressive art society 'Les XX' (The Twenty), where it was purchased by one of the artist's faithful friends. The poet Emile Verhaeren thought it was a marvellous work: 'What joy, what celebration, what jubilant colours unfold across this table at which the woman sits for her meal! Bottles, glasses, plates, lemons, wine and liqueur act upon one another, fill each other with lustre, blend and mingle, yet all the while retaining their triumphant solidity and the rigour of their forms.' Although Verhaeren's description suggests a typically Impressionist painting, there are essential differences between Ensor and the French Impressionists. His vision of light, his focus on the physicality of things and the gusto with which he handles the paint are all primarily Flemish characteristics.

The White Cloud, 1884.

James Ensor was born in Ostend on 13 April 1860. His father was English and his mother Flemish. He trained in Ostend before enrolling at the Academy of Fine Art in Brussels, where he remained from 1877 to 1880. Moving back to Ostend in 1880, he stayed there for the rest of his life. He lived and worked in the oppressive atmosphere of his parental home, where his mother ran a souvenir and curiosity shop.

He first showed his work in public in 1881 at 'La Chrysalide', a progressive art society, where his contributions included *Bourgeois Drawing Room*. In the space of two years, he painted a brilliant series of intimate interiors that evoke a sombre world, into which light gradually begins to penetrate. The painting *Woman Eating Oysters*, which displays a much brighter palette, was rejected by the Antwerp Salon in 1882. It was the first in what was to be a series of rejections by the leading artistic societies and official bodies. Ensor was deeply wounded by this failure to understand his work, yet it was not long before certain commentators at least began to acknowledge him as one of the leading exponents of Belgian Impressionism. *The White Cloud* testifies to his sense of nuance and shifting light.

Around 1885 he began to explore the expressive and decorative potential of light, line and colour in fascinating etchings and drawings like *The Cuirassiers at Waterloo*. The symbolic, dematerialised light of the drawings also crossed over into his paintings.

In the meantime, Ensor's work shed its apparent tranquillity once and for all. Frightening masks and skeletons took over his canvases. These weird images were undoubtedly inspired by Ostend's popular carnival and by the seashells, masks and Chinese curios in his mother's shop. In grandiose creations like *The Intrigue*, the mask-people embody the artist's mental torments, fears and frustrations. With his parodies of religious themes, his anarchism and social criticism, Ensor's work posed a constant challenge to the establishment and the art critics he so detested. Ensor is viewed as a precursor of the Expressionists in terms of his themes, his free style of painting and his use of colour.

In 1888, he met the 18-year-old Augusta Boogaerts, with whom he was to form a life-long relationship, even though the couple never set up house together. He was occupied with family affairs after his father's death in 1887, more specifically with the welfare of his mother, his aunt, who lived with them, his sister 'Mitche' and her daughter Alex.

True recognition came around the turn of the century and Ensor was finally celebrated as the pioneer he was. His painting style also changed, becoming lighter and more playful, and he produced a series of refined, poetic still lifes. He remained in Ostend during the First World War. The deaths of his mother and his aunt prompted him to move house in 1917, though he remained in Vlaanderenstraat. According to one visitor, his new home resembled 'an Oriental bazaar or a fortune-teller's waiting room'. He died in his native city on 19 September 1949.

The museum has the world's largest Ensor collection: 35 paintings and 606 drawings. They include a series of key works that illustrate the evolution of this brilliant artist's oeuvre.

Between 1880 and 1890, Ensor moved from gloomy to bright canvases, dominated by the use of pure colours. All trace of tranquillity disappeared from his work: he began to express his feelings of torment with immense freedom in images populated with saints and demons, masks, skeletons, human faces, caricatures, his own self-portrait and Christ. The tone is frequently critical of society and mocking, even sarcastic. Yet there is also tenderness and a searching, poetic sensitivity in some of the works. He gave free range to his imagination in a highly expressive style utilising bright colours and sharp contrasts.

At first sight, the strange company in *The Intrigue* could be mistaken for a group of masked carnival-goers. It soon becomes plain, however, that these dehumanised mask-people are plotting something unpleasant. The red figure with the doll and the Red Indian-like face in the bottom right corner are clearly up to no good – and Death has put in an appearance. Any bystanders would be well advised to get away as quickly as possible.

Woman at the Window 1889   Henry van de Velde 1863–1957
Canvas, 111 x 125 cm

respective shades are then 'blended' in the viewer's eye according to the theory of complementary colours.

Van de Velde spent the period in question at an artists' colony in the country (Wechelderzande in Antwerp's Kempen region). In the space of a single month in the summer of 1889, he painted a series of six canvases on the theme of 'Village Scenes'. His Neo-Impressionist masterpiece *Woman at the Window* was one of them, executed with infinite patience in a highly refined pointillist style. The subtle colours were achieved by 'chords' of yellow, mauve and orange for the light effects of the clothing and by the dominant tonality of adjacent blue and pink dots.

Van de Velde abandoned the pointillist technique two years later, complaining that 'all that soul-destroying fiddling around' was a constant hindrance. His change of heart did not detract from the brilliant results he had achieved in terms of light and mood.

Henry van de Velde was won over by Neo-Impressionism in 1887, when he saw Georges Seurat's *Afternoon at the Grande Jatte* in Brussels. He immediately set out to explore the new technique, which is also referred to as 'pointillism' or 'divisionism'. The pointillist method uses pure colours that are applied on the canvas alongside one another in the form of dots. The

Henry van de Velde was born in Antwerp and trained at the city's Academy. Having worked for ten years as a very talented artist, he abandoned painting in 1894. He went on to enjoy an international career as an architect and designer, and played an important part in the innovations that occurred in architecture and the decorative arts around 1900.

Van Rysselberghe had a highly personal technique. He worked out the most expressive elements, such as the hands and face, in small dots, and the remainder – primarily the background – in slightly larger ones, thereby infringing the Neo-Impressionist principle that all the dots in the composition had to be the same size.

The Ghent artist Théo van Rysselberghe was one of the few painters to apply Neo-Impressionist techniques to portraits. The notion that a sitter could be represented in an individualised and psychologically revealing manner using the technique of divisionism, with green highlights in the hair and blue shadows on the face, both rendered by means of thousands of dots, seemed inconceivable and even ludicrous at

the time. Yet that is precisely what Van Rysselberghe achieved, making an important and original contribution to Neo-Impressionism in the process.

His portraits chiefly convey the visible aspect of the sitter's personality – the subject's 'presence'. Van Rysselberghe was not particularly interested in the stirrings of his models' souls. He used calm, bright compositions with an almost musical lightness, in which his subjects are usually surrounded with objects from their everyday life, culture or profession to enhance the insight into their psychological make-up.

The sitter in this case is Maria Sèthe, who went on to marry Henry van de Velde.

This painting is a good example of the artist's favourite subject – rural life, nature and country people in brilliant sunshine, with no trace of anxiety or sorrow. This image of cheerful harmony between people and nature is typical of his work. It is easy to understand why he has remained one of the best loved of Flemish artists.

Emile Claus discovered the work of the Impressionists in Paris in 1890, reinforcing his need 'to paint light'. He was particularly attracted to the work of Claude Monet, from which he drew certain elements that enabled him to develop his own style. He abandoned blacks and dirty earth tones and brought colour into his shadow zones, but he never allowed form to evaporate in the manner of the French Impressionists. He always retained a certain realism, which is a characteristic of Belgian art in general. His technique consists of small, energetic strokes of pure colour, laid alongside one another.

He is viewed as the master of 'luminism' – a typically Belgian and somewhat late form of Impressionism. His most attractive works, including *Summer*, were painted on the banks of the river Leie at Astene, near Deinze, where he stayed at the appropriately named hunting lodge 'Zonneschijn' (Sunshine).

Louise in Mourning 1894

Henri Evenepoel 1872–1899
Canvas on wood, 79 x 46.5 cm

Henri Evenepoel was one of the
Belgian painters who moved to
Paris at the end of the 19th century
to perfect his art at the creative
fountainhead of French painting.
He was fascinated by the solidly
structured colours in Manet's paintings and by the style of Toulouse-
Lautrec, whose sense of decorative
line and coloured volumes he
shared. His artistic development
was also influenced by a visit to
Algeria, following which his palette
grew brighter and more intense. His
work conveys an innate feeling for
matter and colour.

As a portrait painter, Evenepoel
had a remarkable talent for captur-
ing the inner life of his subjects.
Louise in Mourning is a brilliant
example. It was painted in the
spring of 1894 during his Parisian
period, a few years before his visit to
North Africa. Louise De Mey-van
Mattemburgh was the artist's niece
but also his lover. The couple had a
baby son in November 1894.

Louise leans on an umbrella,
causing her body to turn slightly
and lending rhythm to the painting.
The black veil and high collar draw
the eye to the sad and tired face
above the elongated silhouette. The
background is a kind of straw covering against a yellowish-green wall,
lightening the composition and bal-
ancing the dark mass of the dress.
Shortly before painting the portrait,
Evenepoel wrote to his father:
'What fascinates and obsesses me
about the face is finding its characteristic element, its special, unexpected side.'

Sadly the young artist was only
granted a short time in which to
develop his talent. He died in 1899
at the age of 27.

Eugène Laermans lost his hearing as a child and suffered a degree of isolation as a result. He represented life in the country in a heroic manner, just as Constantin Meunier did with workers in the metal and coal industries (see p.88). Unlike Meunier, however, his tone is pessimistic and tragic. He painted large images of beggars, outcasts and vagrants, who trudge along beneath dramatic, overcast skies. In some cases, he painted crowds as sad, anonymous masses. In others, like *The Blind Man*, he used a synthetic style to present a small number of figures in a frozen landscape reduced to elementary details – a wide sky, the horizon, a wall and a road with a few trees.

Laermans presented the prevailing social issues of the late 19th century in a succinct and powerful way in works with an undeniable emotional charge that may be viewed as precursors of Expressionism.

This traditional image is notable for
the strong degree of stylisation in
the composition, the colour and the
contrasts between light and dark.
This simplification adds a monumental dimension to the painting.
The theme is not really typical of
Jakob Smits' art, though the pictorial way in which it is executed certainly is.

Smits worked in the Netherlands

The key element of the world he
created in his work is an inner, shap-
ing light, which he viewed as something physical. He used thick, granular masses of paint to give it the
greatest possible intensity. Perspective and shadow gradually disappeared from his paintings. People,
animals and landscapes are all
reduced to their most elementary
form, frequently coming close to
abstraction. In *The Train of the Magi*,
he transforms the thick physicality
of the paint into a raw texture that
conveys an intensely vibrant light –
a light that, in Smits' work, is
invariably associated with darkness.

The museum has a collection of
31 paintings and a great many drawings by this artist.

during the first half of his life, but
then moved to an isolated corner of
Belgium (Achterbos in the Limburg
Kempen, where his house has since
been turned into a museum). He
chiefly painted farming life, the
landscape, portraits and religious
themes, penetrating successfully to
the essence of the underprivileged
rural population, with its deeply
rooted beliefs.

Léon Spilliaert painted a large number of self-portraits in 1907–08 – standing, reclining, reading or working on a drawing. He often portrayed himself in one of the rooms of his parents' house or on a kind of veranda, which he appears to have used as his studio. In this example, he occupies virtually the entire space of the composition. The setting is sober compared to most of

his self-portraits in the period in question, but the image is enlivened by the blue accents in his face and the book and the red ones in the console table. The patch of light on his forehead and hair brings out more strongly his shaded, dark-ringed eyes. He appears deep in thought, a concentrated look that may indicate that he sketched himself in a mirror, or perhaps he is meant to be reflecting on what he is reading. Léon Spilliaert was an Ostend artist who produced a highly individual body of work. It is impossible to place him within any specific artistic movement, although his work has elements of Symbolism, Expressionism and Surrealism. He rarely used oil paints, preferring to work instead with watercolour, gouache, colour pencils and Indian ink, applying limited means and a synthetic style to achieve extraordinary effects. His self-portraits penetrate deeply into what he himself called his 'restless and feverish character'.

The Two Springs 1910

Gustave van de Woestyne 1881–1947
Canvas, 73 x 63 cm

The two women personify life in the city and life in the country. The painter highlights the total separation of these two worlds by having the women stand back to back. One is dressed frivolously, the other simply – they are strangers to each other.

Symbolism of this kind is typical of Gustave van de Woestyne, who belonged to the 'First Latem School', which formed around 1900

together at Latem were looking for a new and meaningful form of art as a reaction to the somewhat superficial spirit of *fin-de-siècle* luminism. Van de Woestyne was a great admirer of the Flemish Primitives and Pieter Bruegel. He developed a pure and mystically charged symbolism that blended dream, mystery and spirituality in rural scenes, religious themes and portraits. His contact with Modernist art led him, after the First World War, to develop an Expressionist style that was more complex than the refined and linear art of his earlier career. The sense of alienation and unreality is, however, a constant in his work.

in the artists' colony of Sint-Martens-Latem – a Flemish village near the river Leie. The poets, painters and sculptors who came

Rik Wouters' only model was his wife Nel. He captured her time and again in fluent oil sketches, water-colours and paintings set in sunny, colourful interiors. The thin strokes of paint are spread across the white canvas as if this were merely the preparation for a painting. Unlike the French Fauvists, however, there is always a structure and a sense of coherence between the colourful patches and stripes. The interiors with Nel are lively images from nature that may be better understood as a heightened form of Impressionism than as examples of Expressionist art.

Nel later quoted some words of Rik Wouters that sum up his artistic vision: 'Achieving your aim with the simplest possible means. Saying a lot with little and making everything clear.'

Rik Wouters was born in Mechelen on 2 September 1882. He trained as a woodcarver in his father's workshop, took lessons in clay modelling and enrolled for evening classes in drawing at Mechelen's Academy of Art. He entered the Academy in Brussels in 1901. Wouters settled in Bosvoorde in 1904 with his girlfriend Nel, his only model, whom he married a year later. He started out as a sculptor before beginning to paint in 1907. His discovery of Cézanne and Renoir prompted the self-taught painter to start working with large, transparent strokes of colour, leaving parts of his canvas unpainted in order to heighten the light effects. Wouters painted flowers, still lifes and sunny interiors with Nel in bright, warm tones: *Education* is an example. Bright, sunlit landscapes came to the fore around 1913. The Impressionist touch of his paintings is also apparent in his sculpture. When the First World War broke out, Wouters was called up and sent to the trenches at Liège. Afterwards, mentally shattered and physically ill, he was interned in Zeist in the Netherlands at a camp for fugitive Belgian soldiers. Nel visited him there every day, taking him for long walks. He produced numerous drawings and watercolours during this period. After undergoing an operation in Utrecht to deal with a shooting pain in his face, he left the camp in 1915 and settled in Amsterdam with Nel, which finally allowed him to resume painting. The small brushstrokes of the past now became large patches, with blue beginning to

dominate red. Wouters was operated on again, this time to remove a tumour from his eye, but it was not enough, and it was in this period that he painted his moving self-portrait *Rik with a Black Eyepatch*. He died in Amsterdam on 11 July 1916, having had a third operation a few months earlier. He was barely 34 years old.

Rik Wouters is the most striking figure among the Brabant Fauvists, producing sculptures, paintings, watercolours, drawings and etchings. His work is a celebration of life and love. The museum has 109 of his works, thanks in part to the donation of 58 items by Ludo van Bogaert-Sheid.

Rik with a Black Eyepatch, 1915.

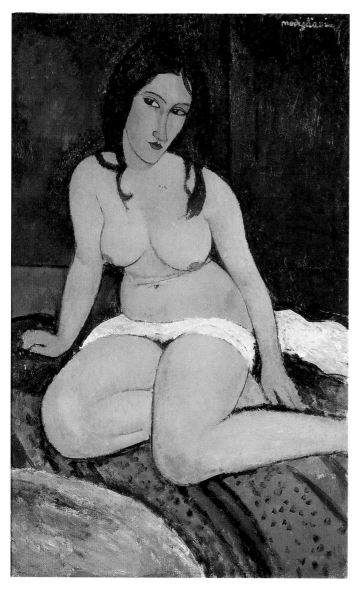

This gentle and melancholy female nude is immediately recognisable as the work of Modigliani. The face is characteristically elongated (the neck less so), reflecting the influence of African and Polynesian art. The almond-shaped eyes, gracefully bowed head and warm, orange-tinged colour of the skin are also typical. In spite of the simplification and the decorative, linear style, the curves of the woman's body are rendered very sensually and almost sculpturally.

Modigliani was an Italian artist who chiefly painted and sculpted the human figure. He worked in Paris for much of his life, often in difficult conditions. He died prematurely of a combination of tuberculosis and drug and alcohol addiction.

Jules Schmalzigaug was the only Belgian artist to respond strongly to Futurism and to incorporate it in his work. Futurism arose in the early part of the 20th century as a reaction against intellectual art and 'moonlight'. It was founded by the Italian Marinetti, who glorified speed, aggression, technology and the city – everything contributing to the intoxication of the modern world. His ideas struck a particular chord in Italy and in Russia. Schmalzigaug discovered the work of the Italian Futurists in 1912 at an exhibition in Paris. His first Futurist work dates from 1913.

Impression of a Dance Hall is a revolutionary, almost abstract painting: its swirls and reflections, rhythm and music are entirely Futurist.

Schmalzigaug was born in Antwerp but spent most of his life in Italy and the Netherlands. A personal crisis eventually led him to commit suicide. He left behind a small body of watercolours, drawings and just 30 oil paintings. His family donated seven works to the museum.

Having experimented with Symbolism and then Futurism, Jozef
Peeters became one of the pioneers
of abstract art in Belgium from
around 1920. He belonged to the
Constructivist strand, in which the
painting is determined solely by
form, geometry and structure. In
1918, he founded the 'Moderne
Kunst' group in Antwerp and was a
great promoter of the avant-garde in
Belgium in the 1920s. He con-
tributed to magazines and organised conferences and exhibitions,
before withdrawing in 1927.

This colourful *Composition*
from 1921 is a painted manifesto.
The properties of its colours create
the impression of overlaid planes,
movement and depth.

The Ostend fisherwoman sits and waits, as robust as a block of stone. She is marked by the tragedy that is inevitably a part of fishing people's existence. The artist was able to witness the harsh life of coastal communities at first hand during his Ostend childhood.

Constant Permeke, son of the marine artist Henri Permeke, is undoubtedly the most monumental of the Flemish Expressionists. He used a sombre, almost monochrome palette of bluish-black and brown tones to create large seascapes and landscapes, imposing fishermen and women, country people and nudes. His vision was grandiose and elemental – rooted in a cosmic experience of life. He found powerful expression in the incomplete, the distorted and even the caricature.

Permeke was among the artists who, in 1942, were prohibited by the Germans from painting or showing their work.

A harmonious impression is created by this domestic scene, with its nuanced colours and Cubist, synthetic style, in which space is reduced to a flat plane. The genial atmosphere is typical of paintings of the Fleming Gustave De Smet. He used a quite rigidly constructed yet tranquil and almost naïve Expressionism to evoke everyday life as he perceived it around him. He preferred warm, often dark, earth tones. De Smet's style betrays the influence of the French Cubist painter Fernand Léger.

A prominent Swiss collector who bought 17 of the painter's works wrote: 'With De Smet it is always fine weather, always Sunday.' Serenity and humanity are, indeed, the main features of this work.

Frits van den Berghe 1883–1939
Canvas, 131 x 141 cm

nately playful and sombre. His formal idiom developed from an extreme Expressionism towards restraint and poetry. In the late 1920s, he set off down the road towards Surrealism.

Fear and obsession are an important thematic element. The dominant feeling in the painting *Life* is one of constriction. The painting evokes the world of Expressionist films in the 1920s – the theatrical figure on the right, the angular architectural forms, the dark and contrasting lighting, the deserted streets and the eerie atmosphere.

Like Constant Permeke and Gustave De Smet, Frits van den Berghe was associated with the 'Second Latem School', which was active just before the First World War in the village of Sint-Martens-Latem on the river Leie. The group laid the foundations of Flemish Expressionism, which developed after the war.

It is immediately apparent from this painting just how much Van den Berghe's personality differed from that of the nature-loving Permeke and the genial De Smet. Van den Berghe was a complex character. He painted carefree rural idylls alongside disquieting and critical works, and images that are alter-

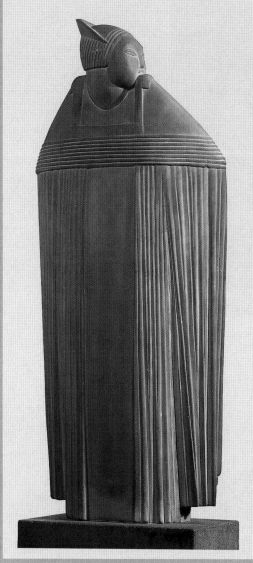

The museum's collection of over 400 sculptures also deserves the visitor's attention. The most important works include the moving *Crucified Christ*, executed at the beginning of the 16th century by an unknown sculptor, and the early 18th-century half-length figure of *Maximilian Emmanuel of Bavaria* by Willem (Guillielmus) Kerrickx (1652–1719), a marble sculptor from Antwerp, who produced work of immense refinement, mainly church decorations. The *Burgher of Calais* is part of the dramatic group of bronze figures that the French sculptor Auguste Rodin (1840–1917) made in 1884–86 for the city of Calais. *The Forgeman* by Constantin Meunier (1831–1905) is a characteristically powerful image of a working man, while *The Kiss* (1881) is a love scene, cast in bronze, by Jef Lambeaux (1852–1908). *The Little Relic-Bearer* (1897) is a symbolic marble sculpture by the Latem sculptor and draughtsman George Minne (1886–1941). Other notable works are *Diana*, a decorative 19th-century figure in ivory and bronze by Josuë Dupon (1864–1935), *The Hooded Cloak* by Oscar Jespers (1887–1970), the impressionistic and more than life-size bronze statue *Reverie* by Rik Wouters (1882–1916) and *The Song of Evil* by Roel d'Haese (1921–1996). The museum also has several typical wooden assemblages by Vic Gentils (1919–1997), whose work combined lyrical Expressionism with sober Cubist design.

Several important sculptures, including Rik Wouters' *Mad Force* and Rodin's *Balzac*, have been loaned to Middelheim Sculpture Park (Antwerp).

Oscar Jespers, *The Hooded Cloak*, 1922, white stone, 89 x 31 cm.

Oscar Jespers was Belgium's leading exponent of Expressionist sculpture. He began his career as an Impressionist, but gradually developed a new form of art, characterised by its simplified, solid, 'Cubist' yet fluid style. In *The Hooded Cloak*, he compacts the human figure into a closed yet elegant form.

Roel d'Haese, *The Song of Evil*, 1964,
bronze, 200 x 87 x 273 cm.

Roel d'Haese is one of the leading figures in
post-war Belgian sculpture. His work consists of Expressionist and Surrealist pieces
executed in metal, and assemblages of various materials. His pronounced interest in
the craft side of art is apparent in the large
equestrian figure *The Song of Evil* – his
most monumental work and the last sculpture he cast himself. It takes a searching
look at human beings – in the artist's view,
their own worst enemy.

The museum bought this painting at the notorious auction of 'Entartete Kunst' – art that the Nazis considered degenerate – at Lucerne in 1939. It is a fine example of the 'Neue Sachlichkeit' (New Objectivity) movement that arose in Germany between the two World Wars. The purpose of the style was to use painting and photography – in other words, the two-dimensional surface – to provide an objective image of social reality. George Grosz was a painter, graphic artist and caricaturist. His highly expressive compositions, which display a far-reaching formal freedom, are often fiercely critical of the abuses and militarism that were rife in Germany at the time. He was one of the founders of Dada in Berlin, and wrote for political and satirical magazines, as did Walter Mehring, the subject of this portrait. Grosz emigrated to the United States in 1933, where he continued his caustic attacks, although these were now directed at the materialism of American society. He played a prominent role in the field of photomontage. His sense of the grotesque made him one of the most merciless draughtsmen of his era.

Pajottenland 1938

Jean Brusselmans 1883–1953
Canvas, 110 x 117.5 cm

Having moved to Dilbeek, near Brussels, Jean Brusselmans frequently painted the hilly landscape of the region, known as the 'Pajottenland', in a style indebted to Expressionism. He translated his impressions of nature into attractively ordered geometric planes, whose vivid colours and lively rhythm give them a playful appearance. He was influenced by the French Impressionists, by Cézanne and Van Gogh, by the Brabant Fauvists and by the Latem Expressionists, all of whose work he assimilated in a highly personal manner. Brusselmans occupied a special place in Belgian art between the wars, with his rigorously constructed canvases, at first brightly coloured and later more sober. The museum has 12 of his works.

Paul Delvaux painted his first Surrealist canvases around 1934, after a brief Post-Impressionist and Expressionist phase. This early Surrealist work, *The Pink Bows*, already contains many ingredients of his highly personal style: theatrically arranged classical buildings in a landscape, somnambulistic naked women, a skeleton and an air of unreality. Other works include deserted stations, lunar landscapes, women in *belle époque* dresses and men in smart suits. The sculptural female type with apathetically staring eyes recurs time and again. Unlike most other Surrealists – Magritte, for instance, and André Breton in France – Delvaux had no time for intellectualism or theories. He simply constructed his own world of dreams and poetry.

Dreams were a key element of the Surrealist movement, which arose in the 1920s. Painters like De Chirico, Dalí, Magritte and Delvaux used a figurative style and a precise, traditional technique to capture their dream images. They juxtaposed objects that cannot normally be combined, lifting things or situations out of their normal context and creating strange associations. Their images often have an inexplicably magical feel.

Paul Delvaux and René Magritte were Belgium's most important Surrealist artists.

with a new and strange perception, in which reality and illusion become confused. This illusionism is the key characteristic of his Surrealism. The 'painting within a painting' was one of Magritte's favourite themes. In some cases, as here, it comprises a landscape on an artist's easel set up on a wooden floor, before an open window or in a field. A 1936 oil painting (in a private collection) and a watercolour from 1938/39 (whereabouts unknown) also have the title *Vengeance* and closely resemble this watercolour. This is not unusual, however, as Magritte frequently painted variations on the same theme – that too was an aspect of his trademark illusionism.

Like the other great Belgian Surrealist, Paul Delvaux, Magritte did not transform reality by distorting it but by combining things that do not belong together. He stripped them – often with a sly wink – of their conventional function and even their name, generating a sense of unease or wonder. There is no point in trying to work out why this watercolour has the title *Vengeance*. The titles that Magritte thought up with the help of his friends were not intended to clarify but to heighten the enigma with the unexpected link between word and image.

A painting of a landscape stands on an easel in a room. The clouds from the 'painting within a painting' float out into the room itself (or at least into the painted image of the room), and even cast a shadow on the wall. In each work, Magritte presents us

Flying Man 1958
Karel Appel born 1921
Canvas, 145 x 114 cm

and Amsterdam (hence the name 'Cobra'). They distanced themselves from the debate about abstraction and figuration, and rejected rational art. They believed more in instinct than in reason, and were more interested in expressing the subconscious than in reproducing the reality around them. They drew their inspiration from the world of primitive peoples, children and the mentally ill.

With its turbulent masses of paint, *Flying Man* is an example of 'action painting' or Abstract Expressionism – a form of painting that, unlike rational, geometric abstraction, focuses on free and spontaneous expression.

Vivid colours, spontaneity and an explosion of raw energy are the key features of this painting and, in general, of the Cobra movement, of which the Dutchman Karel Appel was co-founder. The Cobra group was created in 1948 by a number of artists from Copenhagen, Brussels

The Last Day 1964   Pierre Alechinsky born 1927
Canvas, 330 x 500 cm

This monumental oil painting brings together several normally contradictory strands, such as abstraction with figuration, and spontaneous painting with graphic outlines. Alechinsky intuitively unites them using bright colours and – surprisingly perhaps – a certain restraint. Strange creatures move about in the chaos. According to the artist, the title refers to the idea of death.

The Belgian painter and graphic artist Pierre Alechinsky was a leading member of the Cobra group (see p. 121). After Cobra dissolved in 1951, he continued to develop its spirit in his work. He became interested in oriental calligraphy during a visit to Japan in the mid-1950s, and handwriting and calligraphy subsequently played an important role in his work, alongside the Abstract Expressionist element. *The Last Day* is a fine example. The canvas is the apotheosis of a personal evolution rooted in the Cobra adventure.

LIST OF ARTISTS
AND WORKS DISCUSSED

Snyders, Frans, *Pantry with Dog, Monkey and Parrot,* 68–69

Spilliaert, Léon, *Self-Portrait with Book,* 103

Stevens, Alfred, *The Parisian Sphinx,* 82

Tency, Jan Baptist, *Storm at Sea,* 78

Teniers the Younger, David, *Smokers,* 66

Terborch, Gerard, *The Lute Player,* 73

Titian, *Pope Alexander VI Presenting Jacopo Pesaro to St Peter,* 28

Uden, Lucas van, *The Easterlings' House in Antwerp,* 70

Velde, Henry van de, *Woman at the Window,* 97

Vernet, Claude Joseph, *Seascape,* 78

Vos, Marten de, *St Luke Painting the Virgin's Portrait,* 47

Wappers, Gustaf, *The De Witt Brothers in Captivity,* 79

Weyden, Rogier van der, *Portrait of Philippe de Croÿ,* 15

Id., *Sacrament Altarpiece,* 16–17

Woestyne, Gustave van de, *The Two Springs,* 104

Wouters, Rik, *Education,* 105

Id., *Rik with a Black Eyepatch,* 107

TEXT BOXES

During the preparation of this guide, the author drew a great deal of information from the following publications:

Catalogus Schilderkunst Oude Meesters, Ministerie van de Vlaamse Gemeenschap, Koninklijk Museum voor Schone Kunsten, Antwerp 1988.

Oude Meesters in het Koninklijk Museum, Ministerie van Nederlandse Cultuur, Koninklijk Museum voor Schone Kunsten, Antwerp 1980.

Old Masters in the Royal Museum of Fine Arts, Antwerp 1990

Paul Vandenbroeck, *Catalogus Schilderkunst 14e–15e eeuw,* Ministerie van de Vlaamse Gemeenschap, Koninklijk Museum voor Schone Kunsten, Antwerp 1985.

Y. Morel-Deckers, *Schilderijen uit de 18e eeuw,* Koninklijk Museum voor Schone Kunsten, Antwerp 1988.

Catalogus Schilderijen 19e en 20e eeuw, Ministerie van Nederlandse Cultuur, Koninklijk Museum voor Schone Kunsten, Antwerp 1977.

Maîtres Modernes au Musée Royal d'Anvers, Antwerp 1992

Tekeningen, aquarellen en prenten 19e en 20e eeuw, Ministerie van Nederlandse Cultuur, Koninklijk Museum voor Schone Kunsten, Antwerp 1981.

Beeldhouwwerken en assemblages 19e en 20e eeuw, KMSK, Antwerp 1986.

Aanwinsten 1977–1995, 19e en 20e eeuw, Ministerie van de Vlaamse Gemeenschap, Koninklijk Museum voor Schone Kunsten, Antwerp 1995.

Els Maréchal and Leen de Jong, *The Royal Museum in Antwerp,* in the Musea Nostra series, Crédit Communal, Ludion, Brussels 1990.

Herman Liebaers, Valentin Vermeersch, Leon Voet, Frans Baudouin, Robert Hoozee *et al.,* *Flemish Art from the Beginning till Now,* Alpine Fine Arts Collection (UK) Ltd, London 1985.

Frans Baudouin, *P.P. Rubens,* Fonds Mercator, Antwerp 1977.

De Bruegel à Rubens. L'Ecole de peinture anversoise 1550–1650, exhibition catalogue, Antwerp 1993.

Serge Goyens de Heusch, *L'Impressionnisme et le Fauvisme en Belgique,* Fonds Mercator, Antwerp 1988.

Impressionism to Symbolism. The Belgian Avant-Garde 1880–1900, exhibition catalogue, London 1994.

Herwig Todts, Dorine Cardyn-Oomen, Nathalie Monteyne, Leen de Jong, *Tranches de vie: le naturalisme en Europe 1875–1915,* exhibition catalogue, Antwerp 1996.

Robert Hoozee *et al.,* *L'Art moderne en Belgique,* Fonds Mercator, Antwerp 1992.

I am grateful to the curators and
staff of the museum, especially
Leen de Jong and Erik Vandamme.

All illustrations: © KMSKA (photography: Hugo
Maertens and p. 6 Toon Grobet) and Bridgeman Art
Library London JAL61059 (p. 60).

J. Ensor, L. Spilliaert, G. Van de Woestyne, C. Permeke,
G. De Smet, F. van den Berghe, O. Jespers, R. d'Haese,
G. Grosz, K. Appel, P. Alechinsky: © SABAM Belgium
1999.
R. Magritte: © C. Herscovici – SABAM Belgium 1999.
P. Delvaux: © Fondation P. Delvaux – SABAM Belgium
1999.

© 1999 Ludion Ghent-Amsterdam
Design: Antoon de Vylder, Zandhoven
Typesetting: De Diamant Pers, Zandhoven
Colour separations and printing: Die Keure, Bruges
Translation: Ted Alkins
Editing: First Edition
D/1999/6328/24
ISBN: 90–5544–255–0